THEMATIC UNIT
INVENTIONS

Written by Karen J. Goldfluss and Patricia Miriani Sima
Illustrated by Keith Vasconcelles, Theresa Wright, and Sue Fullam
The authors wish to acknowledge the contributions of Judy Vaden.

Links to Web sites updated regularly at
http://www.teachercreated.com/books/232

Teacher Created Materials, Inc.
6421 Industry Way
Westminster, CA 92683
www.teachercreated.com

©1993 Teacher Created Materials, Inc.
Reprinted, 2001
Updated, 2001

Made in U.S.A.
ISBN-1-55734-232-6

Table of Contents

Introduction 3

Steven Caney's Invention Book by Steven Caney (Workman Publishing, 1985) 5

> *(Available in Canada from Thomas Allen, in UK from Worldwide Media, and in Australia from Transworld Media)*

> > Summary—Sample Plan—Overview of Activities—Spinning Your Wheels—It's a Question of Taste—Invent It! Illustrate It! Share It!—Straw Magic—High Finances—Newspaper Structures—Why Didn't I Think of That?—Innovation Web—The First Computer?

Ben and Me by Robert Lawson (Little, Brown and Company, 1988) 20

> *(Available in Canada and UK from Little, Brown and Company and in Australia from Random Century Pty. Ltd.)*

> > Summary—Sample Plan—Overview of Activities—The Inventor and Me—The Name Game— Mouse-amatics—Mouse House—Poor Richard—We're All Charged Up!—You're Full of Hot Air!—Inventors on the Net

Mistakes That Worked by Charlotte Foltz Jones (Doubleday, 1991) 33

> *(Available in Canada from Bantam Doubleday, in UK from Doubleday Bantam Dell, and in Australia from Transworld Pub.)*

> > Summary—Sample Plan—Overview of Activities—Louis Braille—Inventions Facts and Myths—Piggy Bank Boo-Boo—A Chilling Experience—It Takes All Kinds

Across the Curriculum 43

> **Language Arts:**   What Do You Think?—Making Connections—Step by Step— Fact Pyramid—Poetry Wheel—Sell It Like It Is!

> **Math:**   When Did That Happen?—Time Line Math—If My Calculator Could Talk!—Who's Responsible for This?

> **Science:**   Circuit Folder Game—Tuned In

> **Social Studies:**   Knot Then, Knot Now—Ask the Inventor—Inventor Research Sheet

> **Life Skills:**   Be a Sport—A Frozen Delight

> **Music:**   It's Instrumental

Culminating Activity 66

Bibliography 79

Answer Key 80

Introduction

Inventions contains a captivating whole-language, thematic unit. Its 80 pages are filled with a wide variety of lesson ideas and activities designed for use with intermediate students. At its core are three high-quality children's literature selections: *Steven Caney's Invention Book*, *Ben and Me*, and *Mistakes That Worked*. For each of these books, activities are included which set the stage for reading, encourage the enjoyment of the book, and extend the concepts gained. In addition, the theme is connected to the curriculum with activities in language arts (including daily writing suggestions), math, science, social studies, music, and life skills. Many of these activities encourage cooperative learning. Highlighted in this very complete teacher resource is a culminating activity which allows students to synthesize their knowledge in order to create inventions that can be shared both in school and beyond the classroom.

This thematic unit includes:

❏ **literature selections**—summaries of three children's books with related lessons (complete with reproducible pages) that cross the curriculum

❏ **language experience, poetry, and writing ideas**—suggestions as well as activities across the curriculum

❏ **bulletin board ideas**—suggestions for student-created and/or interactive bulletin boards and displays

❏ **curriculum connections**—in language arts, math, science, social studies, life skills, and music

❏ **group projects**—to foster cooperative learning

❏ **a culminating activity**—which requires students to synthesize their learning to produce a product or engage in an activity that can be shared with others

❏ **a bibliography**—suggesting additional books on the theme

---

To keep this valuable resource intact so that it can be used year after year, you may wish to punch holes in the pages and store them in a three-ring binder.

Introduction *(cont.)*

Why a Balanced Approach?

The strength of a whole language approach is that it involves children in using all modes of communication—reading, writing, listening, illustrating, and doing. Communication skills are interconnected and integrated into lessons that emphasize the whole of language. Balancing this approach is our knowledge that every whole—including individual words—is composed of parts, and directed study of those parts can help a student to master the whole. Experience and research tell us that regular attention to phonics, other word attack skills, spelling, etc., develops reading mastery, thereby fulfilling the unity of the whole language experience. The child is thus led to read, write, spell, speak, and listen confidently in response to a literature experience introduced by the teacher. In these ways, language skills grow rapidly, stimulated by direct practice, involvement, and interest in the topic at hand.

Why Thematic Planning?

One very useful tool for implementing an integrated whole-language program is thematic planning. By choosing a theme with correlative literature selections for a unit of study, a teacher can plan activities throughout the day that lead to a cohesive, in-depth study of the topic. Students will be practicing and applying their skills in meaningful contexts. Consequently, they tend to learn and retain more. Both teachers and students will be freed from a day that is broken into unrelated segments of isolated drill and practice.

Why Cooperative Learning?

Besides academic skills and content, students need to learn social skills. No longer can this area of development be taken for granted. Students must learn to work cooperatively in groups in order to function well in modern society. Group activities should be a regular part of school life and teachers should consciously include social objectives as well as academic objectives in their planning. For example, a group working together to write a report may need to select a leader. The teacher should state and monitor the qualities of good leader-follower group interactions just as he/she would state and monitor the academic goals of the project.

Why Internet Extenders?

Internet extenders have been added to many of the activities in this book to enhance them through quality Web sites. This supplemental information helps to expand the students' knowledge of the topic, as well as make them aware of the many valuable resources to be found on the Internet. Some Web sites lend themselves to group research; other sites are best viewed by the entire class. If one is available, use a large-screen monitor when the entire class is viewing the Web site and discussing its content.

Although these Web sites have been carefully selected, they may not exist forever. Teacher Created Materials attempts to offset the ongoing problem of sites which move, "go dark" or otherwise leave the Internet after a book has been printed. If you attempt to contact a Web site listed in this unit and find that it no longer exists, check the TCM home page at www.teachercreated.com for updated URL's for this book.

Steven Caney's Invention Book
by Steven Caney
Summary

Who invented water skis? How did the zipper get its catchy name? Why is pressure sensitive tape called Scotch tape? Find out the answers to these and many other questions in Steven Caney's Invention Book. *In addition, Caney takes the reader through all the necessary processes involved in marketing and selling an invention. Throughout the book are directions for a variety of homemade projects. Perhaps the most fascinating pages of* Steven Caney's Invention Book *are those which relate the stories behind many familiar products, including Band-Aids, Kleenex, Dixie Cups, and LifeSavers.*

The outline below is a suggested plan for using the various activities that are presented in this unit. You should adapt these ideas to fit your own classroom situation.

Sample Plan

Day 1

- Prepare center and do introductory activities. (page 6, Setting the Stage)
- Read "Getting Started" section of the book. Discuss ideas for new inventions.
- Discuss the invention of the wheel. Make poetry wheels. (pages 48 and 49)
- Learn how to write clear directions. (pages 45 and 46)
- Do the "Why Didn't I Think of That?" activity. (pages 17 and 18)

Day 2

- Read the "Planning" section of the book.
- Make toothpaste and calculate manufacturing costs. (page 7, #3)
- Create Rube Goldberg-style designs and share them in class. (pages 12 and 13)
- Make a crystal radio. (pages 58 and 59)

Day 3

- Read and discuss the "Breadboard, Model, and Prototype" section of the book. (page 8, #9)
- Make a class book of famous inventors. (page 8, #1)
- Introduce the Culminating Activity. (pages 66–78)

Day 4

- Read the "Naming Your Invention" and "Patents" section of the book.
- Role play "Ask the Inventor." (page 9, #5)
- Make a fact pyramid. (page 47)
- Learn about knots and invent a new knot. (page 60)
- Continue Culminating Activity. (pages 66–78)

Day 5

- Read the "Marketing Your Invention" section of the book.
- Practice using an abacus. (page 9, #8)
- Create a new ice cream. (page 64)
- Introduce and practice advertising techniques. (page 8, #10)
- Continue Culminating Activity. (pages 66–78)
- Learn about the abacus and history of computers. (page 9, #8)

Day 6

- Read some or all of the "Great Invention Stories" section of the book.
- Invent with straws. (page 9, #7)
- Read about the invention of roller skates. Experiment with bearings. (page 10)
- Continue Culminating Activity. (pages 66–78)

Overview of Activities

Setting the Stage

1. Prepare a center or touch table full of everyday items that were invented (accidentally or intentionally) to make our lives a little easier. Such items as drinking straws, Velcro®, and permanent press fabric will provide a springboard for discussion and investigation as students read the book.

2. Provide building materials, such as Legos®, Tinker Toys®, and straws for students to manipulate and use for designing new structures.

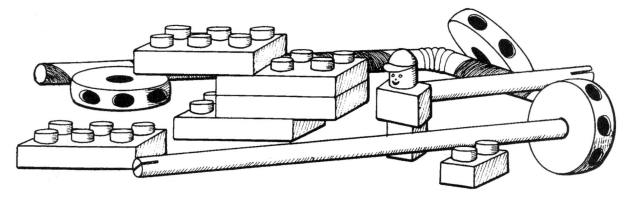

3. Have the students write a fictional account of how ballpoint pens, Dixie® cups, zippers, tea bags, boxes of Kleenex®, or Frisbees® were invented. Ask students to share their stories. After reading *Steven Caney's Invention Book,* compare the students' ideas with the actual stories behind each invention.

4. Introduce one or more of the following activities to pique students' interest in the world of inventions.

    *   Have students sip lemonade through a straw or eat a bowl of corn flakes as you explain the origin of paper straws and Kellogg's first breakfast cereal.

    *   Give each student a LifeSaver® to enjoy as you tell the class about the origin of this ever-popular candy.

    *   As a class, prepare a favorite cookie recipe that calls for chocolate morsels.

    *   Wear ear muffs, plaster your arms with Band-Aids® or roller skate to the front of the room and then tell students about the origins of these inventions.

Enjoying the Book

1. Ask the students what they think it takes to be an inventor. List their ideas. Reproduce and distribute copies of page 43. Discuss the famous quotes and their meanings. How do these quotations apply to the inventor in all of us?

    Brainstorm the steps in the invention process. Have the students determine the correct order of the steps and then rank the steps according to importance. Discuss what might happen if one of the steps was left out.

Overview of Activities *(cont.)*

Enjoying the Book *(cont.)*

2. Define and discuss some terms such as business plan, market research, competition, breadboard, model prototype, and record keeping. Use *Steven Caney's Invention Book* to research and check the brainstorm list and the definitions.

3. Make toothpaste using the ingredients and directions on page 11. Have students experiment to improve the flavor. Discuss the students' ideas on packaging the product. After they have completed the activities on page 11, allow the students to sample the various flavors the class invented. (For purposes of hygiene, use separate utensils or containers for each student.) Ask students to calculate the cost of manufacturing the toothpaste using the information on page 15.

4. Discuss the invention of the Eskimo Pie®. Divide the class into teams of two. Make ice cream using the directions on page 64. Ask teams to invent (and possibly test) ways of preparing a different flavor of the ice cream they made. What other food item(s) could they add to make a new kind of ice cream treat?

5. An inventor needs to provide very specific information, steps, directions, and procedures when selling his or her invention or applying for a patent. Talk about the importance of providing clear directions for any activity. Then ask students to complete pages 45–46. Have students share their results with the class.

6. Research the invention of the phonograph by Thomas Edison. Discuss the story of the jukebox in *Steven Caney's Invention Book* and compare these early inventions to the advances that have been made in audio technology. To help students appreciate this growth, have them make the simple crystal radio on pages 58-59.

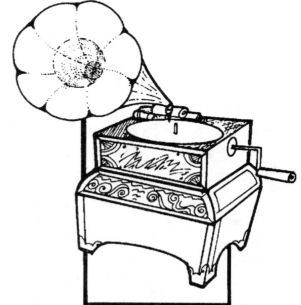

7. One of the most important inventions was the wheel. The wheel first appeared in the Middle East more than 5000 years ago. It has been the foundation for countless inventions and has undergone centuries of modifications and improvements by many people. Have students research the invention of the wheel and the many products whose components include the wheel. Assemble the poetry wheel on pages 48–49. Inside the wheel, write poems about the invention or the many uses of the wheel.

Overview of Activities *(cont.)*

Enjoying the Book *(cont.)*

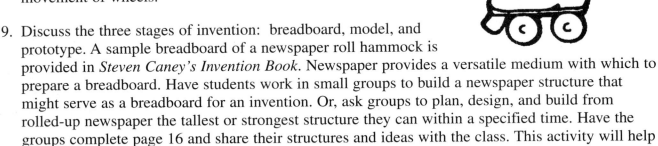

8. Read Steven Caney's description of the invention of roller skates. Have students try the experiment on page 10 to discover the advantage of using ball bearings to improve the speed and movement of wheels.

9. Discuss the three stages of invention: breadboard, model, and prototype. A sample breadboard of a newspaper roll hammock is provided in *Steven Caney's Invention Book*. Newspaper provides a versatile medium with which to prepare a breadboard. Have students work in small groups to build a newspaper structure that might serve as a breadboard for an invention. Or, ask groups to plan, design, and build from rolled-up newspaper the tallest or strongest structure they can within a specified time. Have the groups complete page 16 and share their structures and ideas with the class. This activity will help prepare students for the culminating activity on pages 66–78.

10. Advertising an invention or product is an important part of the marketing process. Reproduce and distribute copies of pages 50–51 to students. Introduce several of the advertising techniques to the class. Allow them to experiment with some of the techniques listed. Have students share their ads with the class.

Extending the Book

1. Have students write a report about a famous inventor. Assemble all reports into a class book titled "I Invented . . ." or "Incredible Inventors." Add the book to your class library.

2. Ask students to explore ways to use ordinary items in an extraordinary way with "Why Didn't I Think of That?" (page 17) and the Innovation Web (page 18).

3. Create a Rube Goldberg-style design to invent a new way to complete a task using the items and directions on pages 12–13.

4. Discuss the statement, "Necessity is the mother of invention," as it relates to some of the inventions in *Steven Caney's Invention Book*. Brainstorm a list of inventions to which this statement applies. Place the list on a classroom chart and have students illustrate the examples. Divide the class into small groups. Ask each group to think of a need in society. Have each group suggest an invention that will help meet that need. Ask groups to present these invention ideas to the class and tell how they were inspired out of necessity.

Overview of Activities *(cont.)*

Extending the Book *(cont.)*

5. Assign, or have students choose a famous inventor to study. A list of inventors is provided on page 61. Distribute copies of the Inventor Research Sheet on page 62 for students to use as a research guide. Create a role-playing situation in which students take turns as the inventor they have been assigned and respond to the interviewers' (the class') questions as they "Ask the Inventor."

6. Have students make a Fact Pyramid. They may use information from an inventor or invention they have studied in the unit. Make copies of the pyramid on page 47. Follow the directions for assembling the pyramid. Have students display their Fact Pyramids on their desks or at a center. Or, hang the pyramids around the room for others to read and enjoy.

7. Read about the invention of the drinking straw in *Steven Caney's Invention Book*. Brainstorm a list of some products that use the scientific principle that makes a straw work. Distribute copies of page 14 and encourage students to try the science and art activities involving the use of the common drinking straw.

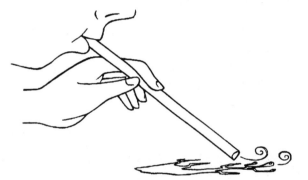

8. The abacus is introduced in "The Story of the Computer." It is considered by many to be the forerunner of modern computers. Bring in one or more abacuses and allow students to practice computations using the directions on page 19. Have the students visit the Web site listed on page 19 to learn more about the abacus. Have them visit the History of Computers Web site.

9. The knot, invented thousands of years ago, is still an important tool today. Brainstorm a list of products and activities that require the use of the knot. Provide each student with a length of rope or twine. Distribute a copy of page 60 to your students and encourage them to try making the knots shown on the page. Have them invent knots of their own and share their inventions with the class.

Spinning Your Wheels

Did you ever wonder why roller skates or skateboards seem to glide so smoothly along the ground?

Roller bearings placed inside the wheels help to create this gliding motion. A bearing is a machine part that helps reduce friction between sliding or rotating parts. The machine parts can then move more smoothly. In a way, you could think of the bearing as an invention within an invention! After reading about the invention of roller skates in *Steven Caney's Invention Book,* experiment with two kinds of bearings—roller bearings and ball bearings—to see how they help to make the roller skate and other inventions work.

Roller Bearings

The roller bearing reduces friction by changing the sliding motion between parts into a rolling motion. Roller bearings use cylinder-shaped rollers.

To show how a roller bearing works to reduce friction between moving parts, try this experiment.

- Wrap string around a large book, such as a textbook, as shown in the illustration. Attach the end of the string to a spring balance. Place the book on a table or desk and pull the book and the scale toward you. Note the reading on the scale.

- Now place several round pencils underneath and beside the book. Pull the book along the table or desk again. Read the scale this time and note the difference between the reading before and after the use of the pencils (rollers). Was it easier to pull the book with the rollers or without them? What effect does the use of the rollers have on friction?

Ball Bearings

Ball bearings are found in bicycle wheels and many fast-moving machines. Instead of a roller, this kind of bearing uses a ball-shaped part to help reduce friction and increase the speed of the moving parts.

To discover how ball bearings work, try the following experiment.

You will need about six marbles, a textbook, and an empty can that has a rim. (A paint can works well.)

- First, place the book on top of the can. Try spinning the book. What happens?

- Now, place the marbles in the groove along the rim of the can. (The marbles serve as ball bearings.) Next, put the book on top of the marbles and gently spin the book around. Is it easier to spin the book with or without the marbles beneath it? Why?

10

It's a Question of Taste

When Dr. Wentworth Sheffield and his son invented the first toothpaste, it was not as successful as they had hoped—until the packaging of the product improved. Today, we can buy toothpaste in a variety of containers, each designed to please a different group of people. However, the consumer, lured by the fancy or clever packaging, will soon turn to another product if what's inside the package does not satisfy him or her.

Think about what you like or dislike about the various brands of toothpaste on the market. How would you improve them? Now put your ideas in motion by making your very own toothpaste.

Begin with the basic toothpaste recipe below and add your own flavoring to it. Design a container and packaging for your new invention, and give your toothpaste a catchy name.

Basic Recipe

In a bowl, mix 2 tablespoons (30 mL) of salt with $2\frac{1}{2}$ ounces (75 mL) of water. Add two cups (500 mL) of baking soda and mix ingredients into a paste.

Try a small taste of your homemade toothpaste. How does it taste? Brainstorm ideas for making the toothpaste taste better. Decide on one or two flavors you might add to improve the flavor. Try each idea. On the lines below, write about what you did and how the new flavor tastes.

_____

_____

_____

_____

_____

_____

_____

Invent It! Illustrate It! Share It!

Rube Goldberg was a newspaper cartoonist. He was famous for his cartoons of wild and complicated inventions. The illustrated designs of his cartoon character, Professor Lucifer G. Butts, represented what Steven Caney calls "additive design." Professor Butts loved to create inventions to make life easier. His inventions performed simple tasks—like turning on the radio—in the most complicated way possible!

However silly or impractical his inventions may seem, designing an invention in this way can be fun and gets your imagination and creativity going.

Create an invention that will perform a task, such as helping you to clean your room. Include some of the parts listed below in your invention.

On page 13, illustrate your invention using a style similar to Rube Goldberg's. Beneath the illustration, write a brief explanation of how your invention works.

List of Parts

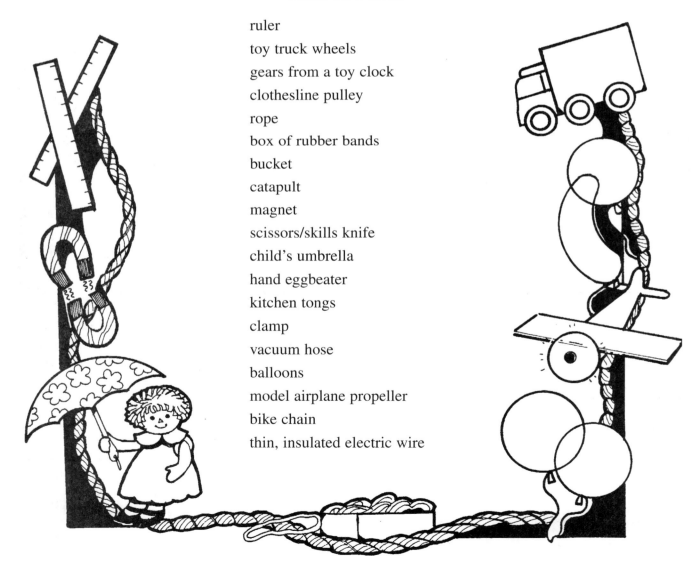

ruler

toy truck wheels

gears from a toy clock

clothesline pulley

rope

box of rubber bands

bucket

catapult

magnet

scissors/skills knife

child's umbrella

hand eggbeater

kitchen tongs

clamp

vacuum hose

balloons

model airplane propeller

bike chain

thin, insulated electric wire

Invent It! Illustrate It! Share It! *(cont.)*

Directions: In the box below, illustrate the invention you created from the list of items on page 12. Give your invention a title. Describe how your invention works and what task it will perform.

(Title)

Straw Magic

The drinking straw may not be a very important invention to many people, but it is one of many ideas which help make life a little easier. Although the drinking straw was designed for a specific purpose, you can use it for art and science projects, too. Encourage students to try some of the "Straw Magic" activities below to learn more about the properties and versatility of this invention.

Straw Painting

Give each student a piece of white construction paper, two or three colors of poster paint, and a plastic straw. Have the students put a small amount of paint (one color at a time or all colors at once, each in different areas) on the paper. Place one end of the straw close to some of the paint. Have students blow through the other end of the straw and enjoy the variations of design and color they produce in their straw paintings.

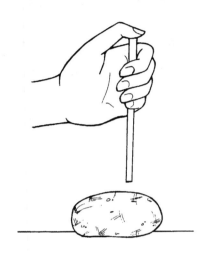

Straw Power

How strong is a straw? Have students try poking a potato with a plastic straw! Now, soak a thin-skinned potato in water for about five minutes. Dry it off. Grasp a straw firmly in your hand (as shown). Place the potato in your other hand and line up the straw at a right angle to the surface of the potato. Jab the straw into the potato. The straw must be at a right angle and should be pushed in with enough force to penetrate the potato. If done correctly, the straw will go right through the potato without bending!

Straw Structure

Provide students (or student groups) with a handful of straws, some tape or clay, and a work surface. Allow them to use their imaginations to design a structure, such as a bridge or tower, that will conform to an established standard—strength or size of the structure, for example. Display the finished structures and ask students to explain how they planned and built them.

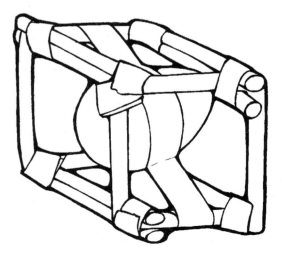

Egg Drop

Divide the class into groups. Give each group the following materials: sixteen plastic drinking straws, three 1-yard (1 meter) lengths of masking tape, scissors, and one raw egg.

Ask each group to create a device that will prevent a raw egg, dropped from a height of ten feet (3 meters), from breaking. The groups can use only the materials provided and may design any type of structure they think will result in a successful egg drop. After a specified time limit has been reached, ask group members to demonstrate their egg-drop creations. Cover the floor with plastic to catch any egg-dropping mishaps!

14

High Finances

Steven Caney's Invention Book

If you were to sell the new toothpaste you invented on page 11, how much would you charge (i.e., the retail price)? To help you better understand how the retail price of an item is determined, do the calculations at the bottom of the page. Then complete the advertisement below.

Try Our New

_____

Name of Toothpaste

On sale for the first time today for only

_____

(Retail Price)

Use the example of the cost calculations for the "Newspaper Hammock" in *Steven Caney's Invention Book* to calculate the retail price of an invention. To determine how much to charge for your toothpaste (the retail price), use the amount provided in step 1 to complete the remaining steps.

1. Start with a retail perceived value of $2.00. You can decide on a reasonable value (price) for your toothpaste by considering such things as how quickly it gets used up, the cost of similar toothpastes on the market, etc.

   Retail perceived value = $2.00

2. Now divide the retail perceived value (from step 1) by 5. This is the amount the product should cost to manufacture.

   The cost of manufacturing the toothpaste is _____ .

3. Next, total the retail costs of the materials you used for your toothpaste. For this activity, let's use a total retail cost of $1.00.

4. To find out what the manufacturer will probably have to pay for the items needed to produce the toothpaste, divide the total retail cost (from step 3) by 4. The manufacturer's cost of materials will probably be _____ .

5. To find the total cost of materials and labor, add the cost of materials (from step 4) to the cost of labor. (The cost of labor is usually about equal to the cost of materials.) The total is _____ .

6. To calculate the retail price, multiply the total from step 5 by 5. The retail price is _____ .
   There are other things that must be considered in the final pricing of an item. These are just a few.

Newspaper Structures

Inventions are sometimes the result of an inventor's creativity in applying a new use to an old idea or product. When designing a breadboard or model, the inventor may use everyday items or objects that were part of another product.

Newspaper is a handy building material that can be used to design all kinds of structures or products that perform a function. Rolled newspaper is quite strong and versatile. In *Steven Caney's Invention Book,* rolled newspaper is transformed into a duster, a watering device, a bottle opener, and even a hammock!

Activity

Here is your chance to be an inventor. For this activity you will use only newspaper and tape. Work in a small group to brainstorm ideas for a structure in which you will use rolled pieces of newspaper. Think of a use for your invention. Then build the structure. In the box below, draw a picture of your finished newspaper structure. At the bottom of the page, write a brief explanation of how you built your invention and what it is designed to do. Share your newspaper structure with the class.

Why Didn't I Think of That?

When an inventor looks at something, he or she sees beyond the ordinary to the extraordinary. The successful inventor tries ideas that no one has ever thought of before, no matter how strange or impractical they may seem. Inventors often find new ways of improving upon someone else's invention. They may find a new use for an old idea or product. Sometimes the inventor combines existing inventions or materials to create something new and unique.

Use your imagination to see beyond the common uses of the following items. Look at the items in the boxes below. Brainstorm with a partner to find as many new uses as you can for the items listed. Then, select an item (or items) from one of the boxes to use for the Innovation Web on page 18. (The last box is empty. You may use it to write your own items.) Cut out the box and glue it in the center of the web. Write your ideas about new uses for the item(s) you chose inside the sections of the web. On a separate sheet of paper, illustrate one of the ideas from the web. Share your web with the class.

a brick, shoelaces, and cups	2 paper cups and a rubber band	plastic jug and string
straws, modeling clay, toothpicks	a jar lid and plastic soda rings	a length of chain, a tire, and a broom
a pie tin and clothes hanger	empty paper towel tubes, tape, and a tin can	*(my choice)*

Innovation Web

See page 17 for directions.

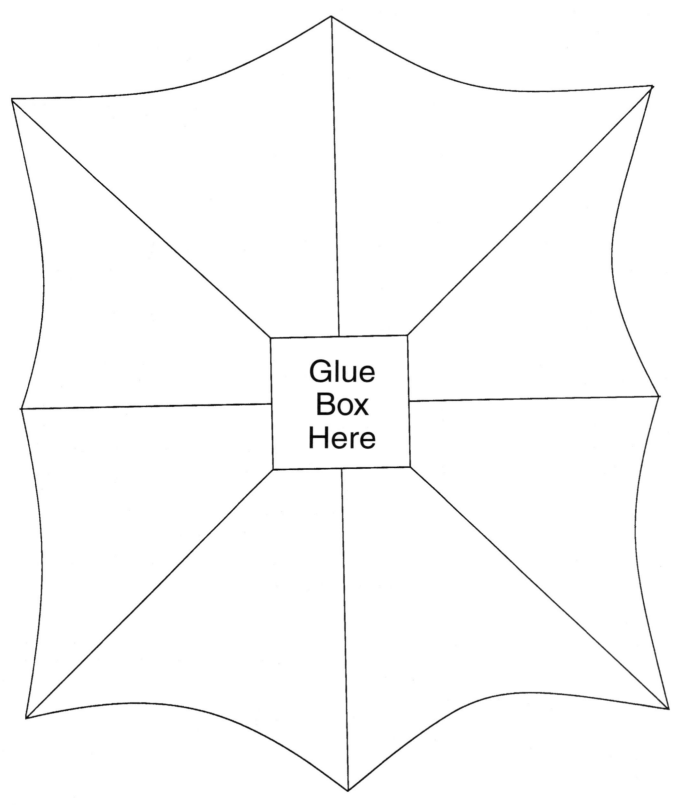

The First Computer?

We live in the "Computer Age." Although people think of the computer as a new invention, machines which compute have been around for hundreds of years. Read about some of the early computers in *Steven Caney's Invention Book*. The author refers to the abacus as possibly the first computer.

An *abacus* is an ancient counting and calculating device created in China, where it is called a *suanpan*, meaning counting board. The abacus has columns of counting beads separated by a crossbar. The beads equal 5 units each above the bar and 1 below. By moving the beads up and down and along the columns, mathematical calculations can be made.

Abacus

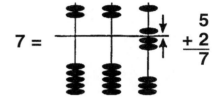

Look at the drawings below to see how it is used to count.

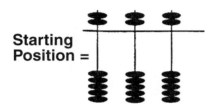 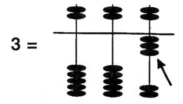 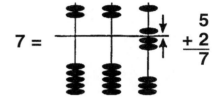

Now let's try some simple arithmetic. To add 25 + 12, place 25 on the abacus. Then, without clearing the beads, add 12 more. Look at the sum. Does it show 37?

Step 1: Move the beads to show 25.

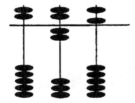

Step 2: Add 2 to the 1s column, which makes 7. Add 1 ten to the 10s to make 30. When these numbers are added together, the total becomes 37.

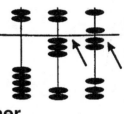

Internet Extender

Introduction to the Abacus
http://www.ee.ryerson.ca:8080/~elf/abacus/intro.html
Activity Summary: Read the information on this Web page about the abacus and then click on *Back to the index* at the bottom of the page. Follow the links in the index to learn about the history of the abacus and how to add and subtract using this early calculator.

History of Computers 1936-1985
http://inventors.about.com/education/inventors/library/blcoindex.htm
Activity Summary: Follow the links from this Web site to read the exciting history of the computer, from the first programmable computer invented in 1936 by Konrad Zuse, to Microsoft Windows in 1985.

Ben and Me
by Robert Lawson

Summary

Benjamin Franklin led an interesting and useful life. As a printer, writer, editor, and publisher, he reached many people throughout the country and the world. His inventions made life easier and safer for others. His scientific discoveries opened new worlds of knowledge about the nature of electricity. As a statesman and diplomat, Franklin was a major factor in the United States' victory in the Revolutionary War. He led a multifaceted life that was full of excitement.

But, according to Robert Lawson, he did not accomplish all of his great achievements alone. In Ben and Me, *we discover that a mouse named Amos played an instrumental part in Franklin's success. You will be surprised by all Amos helped him do.*

The outline below is a suggested plan for using the various activities presented in this unit. You should adapt these ideas to fit your own classroom situation.

Sample Plan

Day 1

- Brainstorm what students know about Benjamin Franklin. (page 21, Setting the Stage, #1)
- Read and discuss the foreword.
- Read chapters 1–3.
- Have students play The Name Game. (page 24)
- Begin plans for a Mouse House. (page 26)
- Make a Circuit Folder Game. (pages 56–57)

Day 2

- Read chapters 4 through 6.
- Work on Poor Richard (pages 27 and 28) and then visit the Web site to learn more about Benjamin Franklin and his Poor Richard sayings.
- Continue working on a Mouse House. (page 26)
- Begin first two experiments with We're All Charged Up! (pages 29–30)
- Add to Ben Franklin knowledge list. (page 27, Setting the Stage, #1)
- Share Circuit Folder Games. (pages 56–57)
- Continue Culminating Activity. (pages 66–78)

Day 3

- Read chapters 7 through 9.
- Complete We're All Charged Up! activity, "To the Rescue." (page 30)

- Have students fly kites.
- Continue work on a Mouse House. (page 26)
- Work on Mouse-amatics. (page 25)
- Continue Culminating Activity. (pages 66–78)

Day 4

- Read chapters 10 through 12.
- Begin The Inventor and Me books. (page 23)
- Experiment with You're Full of Hot Air! (page 31)
- Make a battery. (page 28)
- Find out about other inventors. (page 32)
- Continue Culminating Activity. (pages 66–78)

Day 5

- Read chapters 13 through 15.
- Continue working on the Inventor and Me books. (page 23)
- Make a time line of important inventions. (page 52)
- Create new questions for the Circuit Folder Game. (pages 56–57)
- Complete Ben Franklin knowledge chart.
- Continue Culminating Activity. (pages 66–78)

Overview of Activities

Setting the Stage

1. Find out what the students already know about Benjamin Franklin. Write their responses on one half of a chart titled "What We Know . . ." On the other half, write the title "What We Learned." Add to it throughout the unit. Display the chart so it is highly visible. Although the book *Ben and Me* is fiction, it contains many facts about Benjamin Franklin. Help students determine fact from fiction.

2. Read and discuss the foreword. Ask students what the author has done to make it sound like the story really happened.

3. Tell students this book takes place in Philadelphia in the 1700s. Inform students about some history of that time period, including the Revolutionary War. Talk about how life might have been different in the 1700s from what it is like today. Ask students to name things that they think had not yet been invented in the 1700s.

Enjoying the Book

1. Begin reading *Ben and Me*. The sample plan includes suggested reading for each day; adjust the amount according to your students' abilities and interest levels.

2. Have students play the Name Game, page 24. This can be adapted for students to list inventors or inventions.

3. Mouse House, page 26, will give the students the opportunity to plan and create their own mouse house. This activity will take several days. You may wish to have students do the planning in class and make the house at home. Be sure to give students time to share their models with the class. Display them in a prominent location.

4. Directions for making a Circuit Folder Game are provided on pages 56 and 57. Once these are made, they may be reused throughout the year by changing the questions to fit any topic the class is currently studying.

5. In the activity Poor Richard (pages 27 and 28), students will become familiar with many of Ben Franklin's sayings by completing the phrases. Have the students compare their answers with those found at the Web site about Benjamin Franklin. Let students read about the history of computers at the second Web site.

6. The experiments in We're All Charged Up! (pages 29 and 30) will allow students to investigate static electricity. There are three different activities provided on these pages.

Overview of Activities *(cont.)*

Enjoying the Book *(cont.)*

7. Have students bring in kites from home and go fly a kite! Students may wish to attach keys cut from yellow construction paper or other non-conducting material to their kites to recreate Franklin's famous flight.

8. Have students exercise their math skills with the Mouse-amatics activities on page 25. Encourage students to make up their own math problems that relate to the book.

9. Let students write about their own make-believe inventors with the activity on page 23. You may want to reread the foreword from *Ben and Me* to give students ideas for their own forewords.

10. Show students a copy of the Declaration of Independence. Read it and discuss what it means. Look for Franklin's signature. Discuss the other people who signed it.

Extending the Book

1. Ben Franklin was in France when the first hot-air balloon was launched. Have students complete the You're Full of Hot Air! activity on page 31.

2. Have students research various inventors, using the Web sites described on page 32. You may wish to divide the sources and topics among students to distribute the load. When they finish their research, have them share the information they gleaned.

3. Make a time line of important inventions by using When Did That Happen? (page 52). Students may make individual time lines on their own paper, or you may make a large class time line that extends around your room.

4. Use the time line to solve the problems on Time Line Math (page 53). You may need to provide students with examples of how to solve problems 6 and 7.

5. Have students read some of the following books about "little creatures": *Stuart Little* by E.B. White (G.T. Hall, 1988); *The Littles* by John Peterson (Scholastic, 1986); *The Borrowers* by Mary Norton & M. Hague (HBJ, 1991); *Tom Thumb* by Margaret Hillert (HBJ, 1989); *Thumbeline* by Hans Christian Anderson (Dial, 1979); *Frederick* by Leo Lionni (Knopf, 1987); *The Mouse and the Motorcycle* by Beverly Cleary (Morrow, 1965).

The Inventor and Me

Amos, a mouse who lives in Benjamin Franklin's hat, is responsible for helping him invent the Franklin Stove and the lightning rod. Amos later meets another mouse named Red. "Red had come up from Virginia with Mr. Jefferson—in his saddlebag. Like his patron, he was redheaded, a fiery revolutionist, and a great talker." It seems as though everybody had a rodent they could count on for advice.

Imagine you are a mouse or another small critter. Pick an inventor, past or present, and write a story about how you "helped" him or her with the invention. Be sure to do some research so your story is at least partially based in fact.

Red shared many attributes with Thomas Jefferson. In your story, include traits that you share with your inventor. Also include how you met, where you live, and details on what was invented and how.

You may use the cover provided below for your book, or you may wish to create an original one. Fill in the blanks in the foreword provided to fit your story or write your own foreword.

_____
(Inventor's name)

and

ME

written by

_____

Foreword

The following incredible story is a true account of how _____
(invention)
was invented. It was discovered by

_____ . The writing was
(name of person who found the story)
very difficult to read because it was so tiny. It had to be put in a copy machine at 1,000 times its original size in order to be read. It was determined by scientists at a top secret lab that only a _____
(creature)
could have written it. The family of

_____ is not available
(actual inventor)
for comment. Without any further interruptions, I present the story of

_____ and _____ .
(inventor)   (author)

The Name Game

Amos comes from a very large family. In fact, there are 26 children in his family.

I was the oldest of twenty-six children. My parents, in naming us, went right through the alphabet. I, being first, was Amos, the others went along through Bathsheba, Claude, Daniel—and so forth down to the babies: Xenophon, Ysobel, and Zenas.

What if Amos were to marry and have twenty-six children of his own? In groups of four, help him think of names for his children, going right through the alphabet. If possible, try to list names that the other groups might not think of. When you are finished, give yourselves one point for every name listed. Then share the names with the whole class. If any other group has the same name, cross that name off of your list. Give your team a point for every name that has not been crossed off. Add these points to your original points. The group with the most points wins.

A _____

B _____

C _____

D _____

E _____

F _____

G _____

H _____

I _____

J _____

K _____

L _____

M _____

N _____

O _____

P _____

Q _____

R _____

S _____

T _____

U _____

V _____

W _____

X _____

Y _____

Z _____

Mouse-amatics

Amos admits his family of 28 (26 children and two adults) was not very wealthy.

We lived in the vestry of Old Christ Church on Second Street, in Philadelphia—behind the paneling. With that number of mouths to feed we were, naturally, not a very prosperous family. In fact we were really quite poor—as poor as church mice.

Since this story takes place in the 1700s, we can assume that things were not as expensive as they are today. Suppose, however, that Amos and his family accidentally stepped into a time machine that Ben was inventing and ended up in modern day Philadelphia. Since this family is not used to handling large sums of money, help them solve the following problems. Write your answers on the lines provided.

1. A Mickey Mouse film festival is playing at the local theater. Admission is 50 cents for each child, and one dollar for each adult. Bathsheba found a ten dollar bill in a garbage can. How many mice can go to the movie with this money? (There is more than one correct answer to this question.)

   _____

2. A cheese-tasting party is being held at the I Smell a Rat Supermarket. Admission is free; however, each piece of cheese costs a nickel. How many pieces of cheese will the family be able to buy with a five dollar bill?

   _____

3. Amos, Claude, and Zenas accepted jobs at the university's research lab. They are each paid $2.50 per day. How much money will they earn in one week (7 days)?

   _____

4. Amos was starring in the play "Hickory, Dickory, Dock." (He played the mouse who ran up the clock.) He was allowed to invite four family members free of charge. It costs each additional family member 75 cents. The family had twenty dollars. Did everyone in Amos's family get to see him perform? If so, how much money (if any) was left over?

   _____

5. Amos and his family want to go back to their own time. A scientist has offered to fix the time machine for $200.00. Each child has saved $5.00, and the parents each have $45.00. If they put their money together, will they have enough to get home?

   _____

Mouse House

Amos made his home in Ben's fur hat. He was very comfortable there, and he made improvements on it to make it feel more like a home. "There was a small compartment where I could keep a supply of food against an emergency and, of course, a place for sleeping. There was also a peephole at the front through which I could watch where we were going."

What kind of house would you design for Amos? What things have been invented since the late 1700s that Amos would enjoy having in his house? Think of a common item where Amos might want to live or choose an item from the list below and design a dream house for Amos. Draw a design of your house in the space provided. Once you have your sketch, you are ready to make a model of the real thing. Make your model house in a box or use the actual item. Share your models with the class.

Choose one of the following items:

hat	bowl	planter	purse
mitten	hammock	backpack	pan
suitcase	shoebox	carpet square	drawer
cereal box	doll house	boot	basket

Poor Richard

When Benjamin Franklin was 26, he began his yearly publishing of *Poor Richard's Almanac,* a book full of facts and witty sayings called maxims. The almanac was translated into many languages and was popular all over the world. In the book *Ben and Me,* Amos came upon type-forms for the book that were all set up and ready to print. He began making alterations and picking out letters and dropping them on the floor. Below are the beginnings of several of Ben's sayings. Unfortunately, Amos has deleted the rest of them. Use your creativity to invent new endings to Ben's maxims. Explain what each maxim means. When you are finished, copy your sayings into your own almanac.

1. Look ahead or you will find yourself… _____

    _____

    _____

    _____

2. Early to bed and early to rise makes a man…_____

    _____

    _____

    _____

3. A penny saved is… _____

    _____

    _____

    _____

4. Eat to live, not… _____

    _____

    _____

    _____

5. Three may keep a secret if two of them are… _____

    _____

    _____

    _____

Poor Richard *(cont.)*

6. One today is worth… _____

   _____

   _____

   _____

   _____

7. Great talkers, little… _____

   _____

   _____

   _____

   _____

8. A cat in gloves catches… _____

   _____

   _____

   _____

   _____

9. Well done is better than… _____

   _____

   _____

   _____

   _____

10. Better slip with foot than… _____

   _____

   _____

   _____

   _____

Internet Extender

The World of Benjamin Franklin

http://sln.fi.edu/franklin/rotten.html

Activity Summary: Read about Benjamin Franklin at this Web site and then view the Quicktime movie Glimpses of the Man. Return to this Web page to follow the links that describe Franklin as an inventor, statesman, musician, scientist, and other roles. Select Tour of the Ben's Preview Gallery at the bottom of this Web page and then click on the DO button. Read the 26 wise sayings from *Poor Richard's Almanac*. Click on one of the letters to give your own interpretation of the sayings and read those posted by others.

We're All Charged Up!

Benjamin Franklin was fascinated by electricity. The type of electricity which he experimented with is called static electricity. Below you will find some experiments using static electricity.

A Mighty Flake-y Breakfast

Materials

- one shallow paper bowl
- cereal flakes or puffed cereal
- plastic wrap
- transparent tape

Directions

Fill the bowl halfway with the cereal. Cover the bowl of flakes with the plastic wrap. Secure the plastic wrap with tape, making sure that the top portion covering the bowl is tight. Rub your knuckles eight to ten times across the plastic wrap that covers the flakes. The flakes will begin to jump up and cling to the underside of the plastic wrap as if holding on with strong, invisible arms.

Explanation

As you rub your knuckles across the plastic wrap, millions of electrons leave your hand and "pile up" on the surface of the wrap. This creates a strong negative charge (-). Because "like" charges repel, the wrap pushes away electrons into the dry flakes. The cereal becomes positively charged (+), and since unlike charges attract, the positive electrons of the flakes cause them to move toward and cling to the already negatively-charged plastic wrap.

Oh, Give Me A Comb

A comb is a good source for generating static electricity. As you comb your hair, tiny particles called electrons move back and forth between your hair and the comb. This results in the comb and your hair being charged with static electricity. An object that is charged will attract objects that are not charged and objects that have an opposite charge. Try experimenting using a comb, a balloon, and a water faucet.

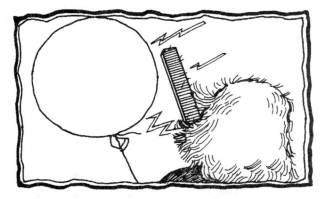

Blow up a balloon and tie it. Hold it next to a comb that has not been charged. What do you observe? Now comb your hair with the comb about 25 strokes. Hold the balloon next to the charged comb. What happens this time?

Turn on the faucet and allow a small stream of cold water to flow out. Hold a "charged" comb next to the water. What do you observe?

We're All Charged Up! *(cont.)*

To the Rescue

After you have completed the experiments on page 29, it is time to put what you have learned to a test. Read the following situation and decide how to solve the problem.

Suzie Shortcut is always inventing new ways to save time. She even mixes her salt and pepper when she buys it so she can put them both on her food at the same time. This worked just fine until Picky Pam came over for dinner. It seems she is allergic to pepper!

Suzie calls and asks you for help. Can you help her?

Materials

- salt
- pepper
- fork
- toothpick
- comb
- balloon

Directions

Mix some salt and pepper together. Using only the materials listed above, can you separate the salt and pepper? (Hint: It may not be necessary to use all the materials listed.) Use the space below to record all of your attempts to solve the problem.

What I Did	What Happened

You're Full of Hot Air!

Benjamin Franklin was in Paris for the first successful hot-air balloon flight in 1883. Many people thought the invention was useless and asked, "What good is it?" Franklin's answer is the now famous quote, "What good is a newborn baby?"

When balloons are filled with hot air, they float because they are lighter than the air around them. Follow the directions below to make your own hot-air balloon.

Directions

Trace the pattern onto tissue paper. Enlarge the pattern first if you wish to make a larger balloon. Lift the rectangular shapes up by folding them along the dashed lines. To form the box shape of the balloon, fold the tabs in and glue to the appropriate sides. Allow glue to dry. Holding the open end of the balloon down, inflate it with the heat from a hair dryer. Watch your balloon rise!

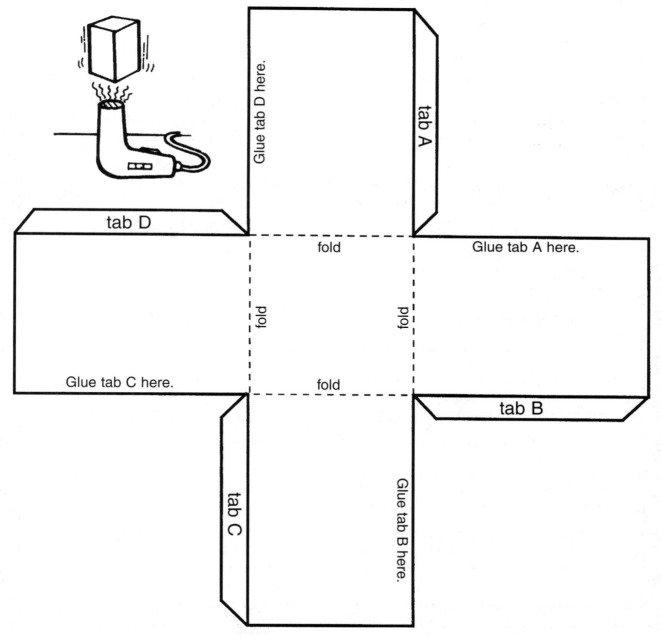

Inventors on the Net

Internet Extender

Have the students visit the Web sites below to learn about inventors and inventions.

Inventor Profiles

http://www.ideafinder.com/facts/fip.htm

Activity Summary: This site lists many inventors, including the following. Divide these among the students to have them gather information and write a profile of an inventor. They should follow the links from this Web page to other Web sites to read and gather additional information regarding their inventor. Each week this site highlights a new inventor.

Alexander Graham Bell	**Grace Hopper**
Henry Bessemer	**Edwin Land**
George Washington Carver	**Tim Berners-Lee**
Leonardo da Vinci	**Guglielmo Marconi**
George Eastman	**Henri Nestle**
Thomas Alva Edison	**Alfred Nobel**
Albert Einstein	**Blaise Pascal**
Douglas Engelbart	**Frederick Winslow Taylor**
Michael Faraday	**Nikola Tesla**
Enrico Fermi	**Earl Tupper**
Henry Ford	**Count Alessandro Volta**
Benjamin Franklin	**James Watt**
Johannes Gutenberg	**Frank Lloyd Wright**
Heinrich Hertz	**Ferdinand Zeppelin**

Inventors Hall of Fame

http://www.invent.org/book/index.html

Activity Summary: Click on Index of Inventions at this Web site to find an extensive list of inventors. These have links to additional information about the inventions and inventors. You can also access links to an alphabetical list of inventors.

Invention Dimensions: Inventor of the Week

http://web.mit.edu/invent/www/archive.html

Activity Summary: When you reach this Web page, you will find an alphabet displayed across the page. Click on any letter, and it will show a list of inventors with last names beginning with that letter. Examples of inventors include Steve Jobs, Steve Wozniak, Hedy Lamar, and Eli Whitney. Have the students select a letter and then click on it and choose one or two inventors to write about. Pictures of the inventors are included.

Mistakes That Worked
by Charlotte Foltz Jones

Summary

Bite into a chocolate chip cookie. Sip a Coca-Cola®. Dip your tea bag while enjoying a breakfast brown 'n' serve roll with your favorite cheese omelette. What do all of these delicious foods have in common? They were all inventions that happened by mistake or by accident. In Mistakes That Worked, *students will learn the fascinating circumstances that led to the invention of fudge, ice cream cones, maple syrup, Popsicles®, potato chips, penicillin, X-rays, Frisbees®, piggy banks, Silly Putty®, bricks, glass, and Post-it Notes®, to name a few. A section of the book is devoted to the mistakes that resulted in the naming of cities and sites around the world.*

Students will be amused and astonished when they learn how Levi® jeans, Velcro®, trouser cuffs, leotards, and Cinderella's glass slipper came to be. Perhaps the most important lesson to be learned from Mistakes That Worked *is best described by Bertolt Brecht in the introduction: "Intelligence is not to make no mistakes. But quickly to see how to make them good."*

The outline below is a suggested plan for using the various activities that are presented in this unit. You should adapt these ideas to fit your own classroom situation.

Sample Plan

Day 1

- Prepare and discuss a bulletin board. (page 34, Setting the Stage, #1)
- Distribute and enjoy chocolate chip cookies. (page 34, Setting the Stage, #3).
- Make "It Takes All Kinds" Invention Booklet. (page 34, Setting the Stage, #2)
- Read some or all of Chapter 1. (page 34, Enjoying the Book, #1)
- Continue Culminating Activity. (pages 66–78)

Day 2

- Read chapter 2. (page 34, Enjoying the Book, #2)
- Brainstorm ideas for making connections between items. (page 44)
- Learn the Braille Alphabet. (page 36)
- Make a display showing mistakes that worked and accidental discoveries. (page 35, #1)
- Continue Culminating Activity. (pages 66–78)

Day 3

- Read Chapters 3 and 4.
- Discuss the invention of the Frisbee®.
- Invent your own game with "Be a Sport." (page 63)
- Make piggy banks. (page 35, Extending the Book, #5)
- Solve math problems and learn facts about inventors/inventions. (page 55)
- Continue Culminating Activity. (pages 66–78)

Day 4

- Read Chapter 5. (page 35, Extending the Book, #2)
- Make a map of places and sites mistakenly named. (page 35, #2)
- Make iced-pops and have a "Chill-Out Party." (page 39)
- Make musical instruments. (page 65)
- Display students' inventions and make Culminating Activity presentations. (pages 66–78)

Overview of Activities

Setting the Stage

1. Prepare a bulletin board of "Foolish Ideas That Changed the World." Include inventions as well as ideas that may have been dismissed as ridiculous by many but whose merits were far reaching. Use the bulletin board as a springboard for discussion. Have students add similar inventions to the bulletin board.

2. Reproduce a copy of the Invention Booklet on pages 40-42 for each student. Have students cut out the pages, arrange them in order, and assemble the booklet. As students read about the inventors and their inventions, focus on the title of each page. Discuss how the invention relates to the title. Ask students if any of the inventions might have been the result of a mistake or an accidental discovery. You may want to assign groups to do further research on each of the inventors/inventions. Prepare a wall chart labeled with the titles used in the Invention Booklet. Add the students' research and illustrations to the chart.

3. Distribute a chocolate chip cookie to each student. (First check for food allergies.) Explain that the chocolate chip cookies they are about to eat were the result of a mistake. Allow students to enjoy the cookies as you read about the invention of the chocolate chip cookie from *Mistakes That Worked*.

Enjoying the Book

1. Read the section titled "Tummy Fillers" from *Mistakes That Worked*. Ask students to imagine ways in which other familiar foods might have been invented. Encourage students to express their ideas for new food products using familiar food combinations—for example, adding a jelly center to a peanut butter cookie to make a peanut butter and jelly cookie. Have students write about and illustrate their ideas.

2. As you read "Doctor, Doctor" with the class, discuss the medical impact of penicillin and X-rays and the events that led to their discoveries. If possible, ask a local physician to speak to the class about other life-saving medicines or medical equipment, including those that may have been accidentally discovered.

3. Discuss the story of guide dogs for the blind. Have students research Louis Braille and the Braille Alphabet. Distribute copies of page 36 and encourage students to become familiar with the Braille Alphabet as they try the activities on the page.

Overview of Activities *(cont.)*

Enjoying the Book *(cont.)*

4. Read the story of the Frisbee® Disc. Have a Frisbee® throwing contest. Divide the class into groups and ask each group to invent a new Frisbee® game.

5. Brainstorm a list of items that students use when playing games or participating in sports. Where possible, have students locate information on how the games or sports developed and how some of the items involved in each activity were invented. Share the research with the class. Distribute copies of "Be a Sport" on page 63. Have students use the suggested list or choose items of their own to invent a new game. Share the new games and rules with the rest of the class.

Extending the Book

1. Make a display representing some of the mistakes and accidental discoveries that became successes. Divide the class into five groups. Reproduce and enlarge the category signs on page 37. Assign a category to each group. Have groups prepare a display of samples and information about some of the inventions that developed as a result of a mistake. Glue the category signs to a piece of index paper or construction paper and place each sign at its appropriate display area.

2. Make an outline map of the world on a large piece of butcher paper. Using index cards, have students write about the places named in chapter 5 of *Mistakes That Worked*. Attach yarn from the cities or sites to the index cards.

3. Expose students to interesting facts about other inventions and inventors as they complete the calculations on page 55. Ask students to locate and share any additional information they may find about these inventors/inventions.

4. While many of the inventions in *Mistakes That Worked* may have begun as mistakes, they were turned into successes because of the inventors' perseverance and ability to see connections among various items or ideas. Distribute page 44. Have students choose two items and brainstorm connections between them.

5. Students will be intrigued with the story of the piggy bank. Have them bring in piggy banks and share observations about the types and designs of each bank. Compare the variety of banks available today with the original "pygg" bank. Have students make piggy banks using the materials and directions on page 38.

Internet Extender

Alexander Fleming
http://www.pbs.org/wgbh/aso/databank/entries/bmflem.html
Activity Summary: Read the brief biography of the man who discovered penicillin by accident.

Archimedes
http://www.mcs.drexel.edu/~crorres/Archimedes/contents.html
Activity Summary: Learn about the inventions of this ancient Greek, including the burning mirror, lever, and Archimedes screw. Click on The Golden Crown link to see that Archimedes' method of checking the gold content in the crown would not work.

Louis Braille

In 1824, a French student named Louis Braille invented a system of raised dots on a piece of paper that could be used by blind or visually impaired individuals. This alphabet was appropriately named the Braille Alphabet. The dots, arranged in a specific way, represent letters, numbers, and punctuation. To become familiar with this system, use the Braille Alphabet below to write a brief letter to a friend.

Braille Alphabet

Internet Extender

Louis Braille

http://www.cnib.ca/braille_information/louis_braille.htm

Activity Summary: Learn about Louis Braille, who was blinded by an accident when three years old and eventually invented a way for the blind to read.

The Six Magic Dots of Braille

http://ww.cnib.ca/pamphlets_publications/sixdots/6dots.htm

Activity Summary: Learn about the Braille six-dot method of recreating the alphabet and numbers. Print a copy of the pages at the Web site and then "read" the Braille version of a phrase from *The Little Prince*.

Inventions Facts and Myths

See page 35 for directions.

Aspirin	Frisbee	Post-It Notes
Automobile	Ice-Cream Cone	Potato Chips
Baby Formula	Internet	Printing Press
Band-Aid	Ivory Soap	Refrigerator
Bible (Gutenberg)	Jigsaw Puzzle	Remote Control
Blue Jeans	Jell-O	Safety Glass
Chewing Gum	LEGO	Safety Pin
Christmas Lights	LifeSavers Candy	Scrabble
Coca-Cola	Lionel Trains	Sewing Machine
Computer Mouse	Liquid Paper	Silly Putty
Cracker Jacks	Microwave Oven	Slinky
Crayons	Milk Carton	Smoke Alarm
Dictionary Words	Nylon Stockings	Tea
Elevator	Paper Towels	Toll House Cookies
Fax Machine	Piggy Bank	Traffic Light
Flashlight	Planters Peanuts	Vacuum Cleaner
Franklin Stove	Popsicle	Velcro

Internet Extender

Inventions Facts and Myths

http://www.ideafinder.com/facts/fsp.htm

Activity Summary: Divide this list of inventions among the students to research several items. Have them make an illustrated report to display on a bulletin board.

Piggy Bank Boo-Boo

The piggy bank is one of the most popular mistakes ever made! It was invented over four hundred years ago when people began tossing spare coins into pots made of a clay called "pygg."

"Pygg" became the name for earthenware, but the term was forgotten over the years. And so, it is not surprising that in the 1800s, when potters were asked to make pygg banks, they designed pig-shaped banks. These new banks became very popular—and the term "piggy bank" was used to refer to coin banks. Today, hundreds of years after the "pygg" bank was invented, coin banks shaped like pigs are still used to save those extra coins for a rainy day. Follow the directions below to make a piggy bank of your own. Then start saving money you may have been given for special occasions or have earned by doing chores.

Materials

- plastic jug with handle (Large bleach or fabric softener jugs work well.)
- markers (permanent)
- craft knife or penknife (Be sure an adult supervises the use of this.)
- felt (optional)
- scissors
- glue

Directions

1. Wash the jug thoroughly and allow it to air dry. Screw the cap on.

2. To make the coin slot, draw a rectangular shape about halfway between the base of the handle and the bottom of the jug. Make the slot large enough to fit the largest coin you intend to slip through it.

3. Use a penknife or craft knife to cut out the rectangular slot.

4. Place the jug on its side as shown in the picture.

5. With a permanent marker, draw the pig's eyes, mouth, ears, feet, and tail on one side of the jug. Do the same on the other side so that the pig's features can be seen from either side. To add more color and texture to the piggy bank, cut the pig's features out of felt and glue them on the jug.

6. Cut out the label below and glue it on the side of the bank.

7. Put several coins in the piggy bank to keep it on its belly and prevent the bank from rolling to one side or the other.

8. To remove the coins you have collected, unscrew the cap and empty the pig.

A Penny Saved Is a Penny Earned

A Chilling Experience

People have been enjoying frozen iced-pops for many years thanks to the accidental discovery of an 11-year-old boy named Frank Epperson. A stirring stick left overnight in a soda water powder and water mixture froze, forming the first iced-pop. Years later Frank Epperson opened a business, producing flavored Popsicles®.

Invent your own iced-pop and give it a name. Start with the basic recipe below. Add your own flavoring. When your iced-pops are ready, have a class "Chill-Out Party."

Materials

- water
- 3 oz. (80 mL) plastic drinking cup
- heavy-duty aluminum foil
- craft stick

- sweetened flavorings made from the juice of cherries, lemons, oranges, fruit flavored powdered drink mixes, etc.
- permanent marker

Directions

1. Fill the plastic cup about two-thirds full of water.

2. Add enough flavoring to give the water a pleasant taste. Stir gently with the craft stick. Remove the stick.

3. Place a piece of heavy-duty aluminum foil over the top of the plastic cup to form a lid. Puncture the center of the foil with the craft stick and push the stick through the hole, allowing it to stand upright in the middle of the water mixture.

4. Place the cup in a freezer until the water mixture has completely frozen.

5. Remove the plastic cup by briefly setting it in warm water until the iced-pop lifts out easily. (Keep the foil on the iced-pop to catch any drips as the pop melts.)

It Takes All Kinds

Invention Booklet

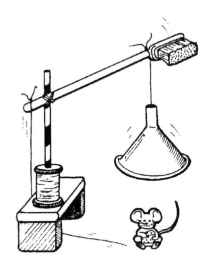

This booklet belongs to

_____

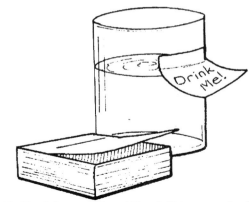

A Failed Invention That Succeeded

Post-it Notes® have become a necessity in the business world. That little piece of paper that can be attached to another and easily removed is indispensable to all who like to add a note to a finished paper. The glue that makes it possible was at first considered a failure because it didn't stay attached permanently. Think of as many uses as you can for the Post-it Note®.

2

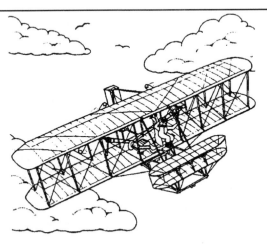

An Invention That Changed the World

The Wright Brothers invented a way to fly. Soon it affected many areas of our lives. Mail traveling great distances could be delivered in a few days. People could travel to places it would have taken months to get to before. In what other ways has the invention of the airplane changed the world?

3

An Invention That Revolutionized Industry

Henry Ford invented the assembly-line method of production. Each person did one part of the whole job. As a result, the car could be built in a much shorter time. In what other areas of industry does the assembly line help in the manufacturing process?

4

It Takes All Kinds *(cont.)*

An Invention That Saved Lives

In the early 1900s, Garrett A. Morgan invented a safety hood that supplied clean air from an air bag attached to the wearer. It prevented suffocation from gases and smoke. In what occupations today do people use protective masks or suits? Why?

5

An Invention by Accident

Rubber was known about for one hundred years, but it became soft and sticky in hot weather and hard and brittle in cold temperatures. Charles Goodyear experimented but couldn't find a solution until the day he accidentally dropped a mixture of rubber and sulfur onto a hot stove. He had found the correct formula! How many products can you name that are made from rubber?

6

An Invention from Observation

Clarence Birdseye was a fur trader who lived with the Eskimos in 1914. He watched them catch fish and store them outside in the frigid, dry air. Months later the fish would be thawed and then cooked. They tasted as if they had just been caught. When he returned to the United States, he began to experiment until he perfected a quick freezing method to preserve foods. What kinds of food products can be frozen? Which products do not freeze well?

7

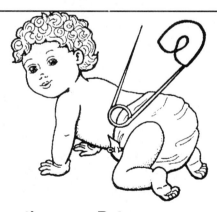

An Invention on a Bet

In 1849, Walter Hunt owed a man fifteen dollars. The man said he would cancel the debt and pay Walter Hunt an additional four hundred dollars if Hunt could invent something from a piece of wire. Three hours of twisting resulted in the invention of the safety pin! Why do you think it was called a safety pin? Can you invent something new from the common safety pin?

8

It Takes All Kinds *(cont.)*

An Invention from Cooperation

At the St. Louis Fair in 1904, two neighboring vendors had problems. One vendor's cookies weren't selling and the other had run out of dishes for serving his ice cream. The cookie vendor rolled his product into a cone and the ice-cream vendor put ice cream into it. And so, the ice-cream cone was born! What is your favorite flavor of ice cream?

9

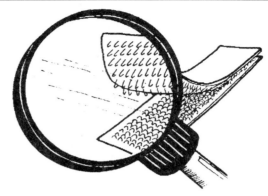

An Invention from Nature

In 1948, George deMestral took a hike in the Swiss Alps. Seed pods called burrs stuck to his clothing. He wondered why and he wanted to know. Looking closely, he saw tiny hooks that clung to the threads in his clothes. Eight years of working resulted in Velcro,® a fastener used today for everything from shoes to hanging pictures. Name some items with Velcro® attachments that you have at home.

10

An Invention from Vision

Leonardo da Vinci invented a helicopter four hundred years before it was possible to build it. The helicopter, and da Vinci's invention of a parachute and an ornithopter, existed only as drawings because the materials and equipment to build them did not exist during da Vinci's lifetime. Design a mode of transportation for the future.

11

An Invention by a Child

Chester Greenwood hated to have cold ears! He invented the earmuff to keep his ears warm while ice skating. If you could invent something that would help to make life a little more comfortable for children, what would it be?

12

What Do You Think?

An inventor needs to be creative, imaginative, and willing to explore and develop new ideas. Leonardo daVinci, born in 1452, designed bridges, weapons, costumes, machines, and scientific instruments. He invented (on paper) a parachute, a helicopter, and an ornithopter.

Thomas Alva Edison not only invented the light bulb, he created the business of inventing as well. He encouraged others to invent by setting a goal for his inventors of one new invention every ten days and one significant invention every six months.

Leonardo da Vinci and Thomas Edison, along with many other successful inventors, shared a common attitude about life and the business of inventing. Below are some quotes made by famous people who had ideas that changed our lives. Read each quotation. Write what you think these men meant by their statements. Share your ideas with the class and explain why you agree or disagree with each statement.

1. *Being ignorant is not so much a shame as being unwilling to learn.* Benjamin Franklin

   _____

   _____

2. *Imagination is more important than knowledge.* Albert Einstein

   _____

   _____

3. *99% of the failures come from people who have the habit of making excuses.* George Washington Carver

   _____

   _____

4. *Genius is simply hard work—1% inspiration and 99% perspiration.* Thomas Alva Edison

   _____

   _____

Making Connections

Inventors look at ordinary things and see connections that others may not see. Practice making connections between each pair of items below by brainstorming with a partner ways in which the items are similar and/or different.

Next, choose one pair of items and write your brainstormed ideas in the Venn diagram at the bottom of the page. Share your ideas with the class. You may find that sometimes the connection is not in how they are alike but in how they are different

Connections List

parrot—radio	flower—cat
television—camera	cough—sneeze
pen—pencil	wind—ocean wave
table—chair	valley—hill
ocean—mountain	grass—clouds
rhinoceros—ship	ice cream—soup
lunch—breakfast	pencils—computers

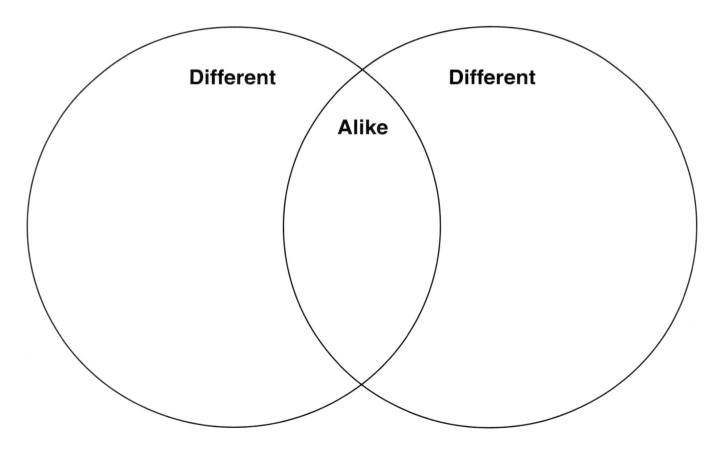

Different   **Different**

Alike

Step by Step

An inventor must be able to give clear directions to ensure that his or her invention can be used by another person. Have the class brainstorm a list of important words needed to give good directions. Words or phrases such as "to the right," "first," "next," "vertically," "in the left-hand corner," and "above" help to clarify directions.

Provide examples of good directions and vague or confusing directions. Discuss the elements of each that reinforce or impede understanding.

Pair off students for the How To's and Copycat activities below and on page 46. When each activity is completed, discuss the problems and successes each team experienced.

How To's

Have each student in a team of two choose something to tell his/her teammate how to do. When the students do this activity for the first time, have them describe it rather than demonstrate it. It may be necessary to practice this activity a few times, but once students are more skilled they can choose more complicated directions, like explaining how to play a game, fix a meal, or perform a chore.

When teams are ready, have one member of each pair of students choose a suggested item below (or prepare your own list) to describe. Remind students to try to give clear, step-by-step directions. Switch roles to allow the other member of each pair to describe an item.

Suggestions: How to...

dial a phone	go to the lunchroom	tie a shoelace
answer a phone	sharpen a pencil	make a bed
make a sandwich	organize your desk	address an envelope
make scrambled eggs	use a key to unlock your door	look up a word in the dictionary
kick a football	catch a fly ball	write in cursive the word "cat"
throw a baseball	turn on (or set up) the computer	find the average of three numbers
brush your teeth	check a book out of the library	wash a car

Step by Step (cont.)

Copycats

Pair off students for this activity. Turn desks or arrange seating so that each student in the pair has his or her back to the other student. Reproduce and cut out the pictures below. Place them in an envelope and distribute them to each group. Give one partner (the illustrator) a blank piece of paper and a pencil. The other student (the describer) chooses one of the sketches from the envelope to describe to his or her partner. (Students may want to use their own sketches. Remind them to make simple line drawings that are easy to explain.) After directions have been given, ask the illustrator and describer in each group to compare the pictures. How similar to the actual sketch is the illustrator's picture?

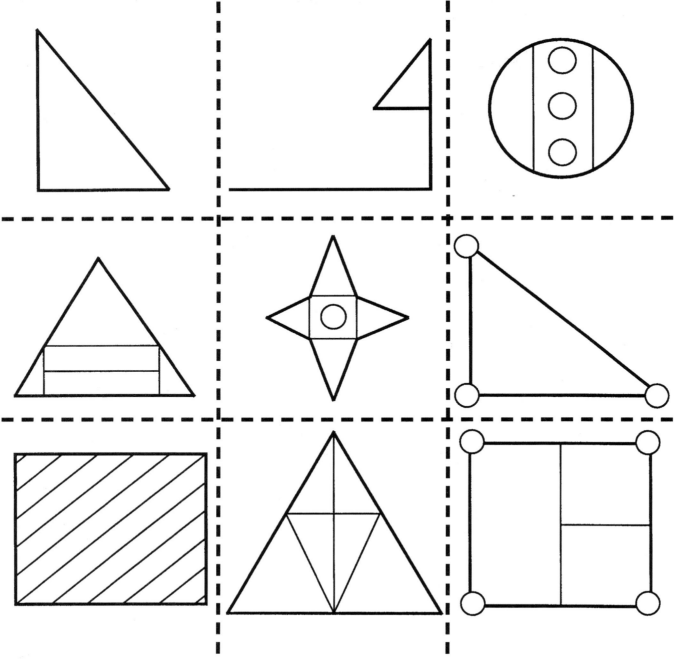

Fact Pyramid

Choose an inventor or invention. Locate interesting and important facts about your subject. On each side of the pyramid, write one fact relating to the inventor or invention. Assemble the pyramid using the directions below. Place facts and illustrations on each face of the pyramid. Share the pyramid with your classmates. Display it on your desk or in a special place in the classroom.

Construct paper pyramids following the directions below.

Materials: scissors; glue or tape; pyramid pattern

Directions: Reproduce the pattern on construction paper or index paper. Cut out the pattern along the solid lines. Fold inward along all dashed lines. Glue or tape the tabs to the adjacent edges making sure that the tabs remain inside the pyramid.

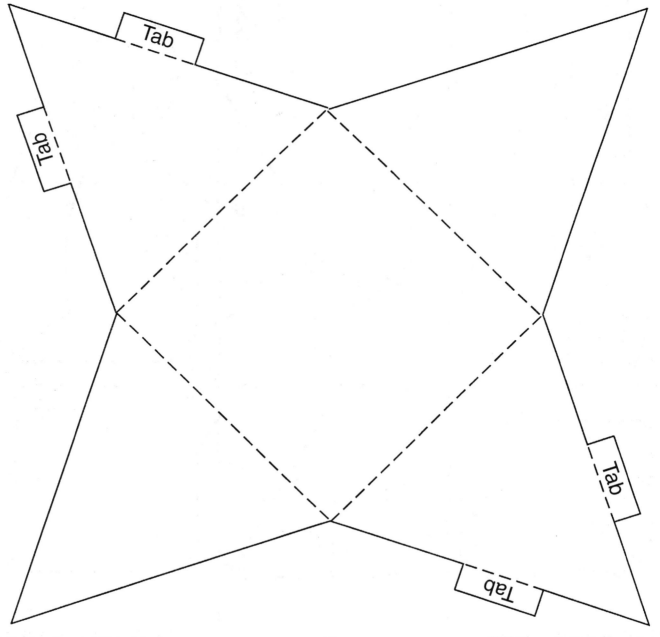

Poetry Wheel

Write a four-line or four-verse poem about the invention of the wheel. Place a different line/verse in each wheel section on page 49, starting with section one. Then, cut out the wheel below. Cut out the one section of the wheel marked "Cut Out." To assemble the poetry wheel, place the wheel on top of the poetry sections, matching the centers of each. Poke a brad through the centers. (To move the wheel more easily, widen the brad hole in the center of the wheel.) Read the poem by moving the open section of the wheel through each section, starting with number one.

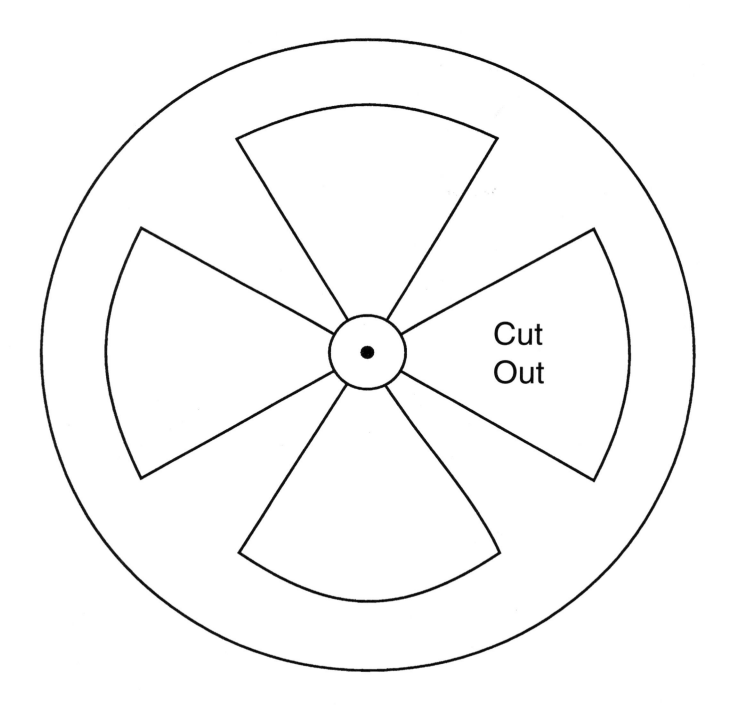

Poetry Wheel *(cont.)*

_____

Poem Title

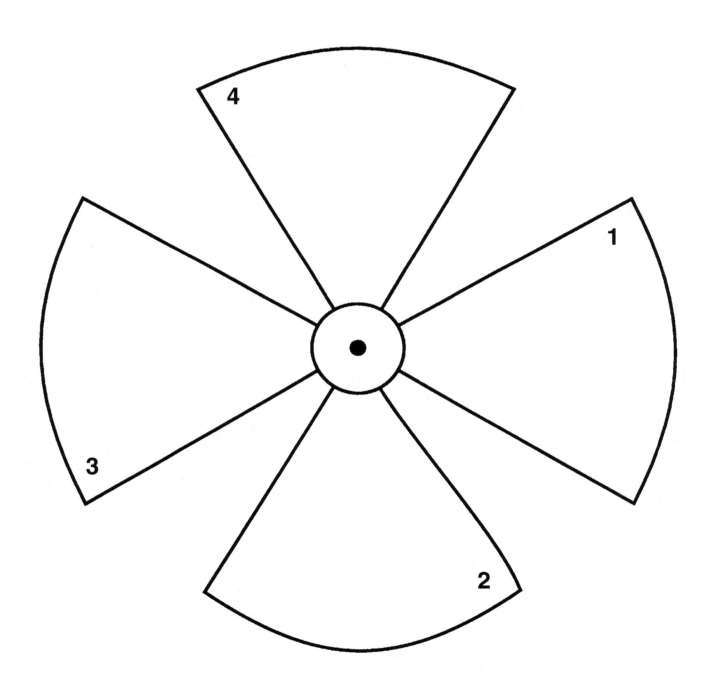

Written by _____

Sell It Like It Is!

If you invented a new product or created a new and improved design on an existing product, how would you let others know about it?

It is an advertiser's job to convince the consumer to buy a product. Consider the advertisements you hear or see on television or radio, and in newspapers and magazines. Which ones seem to be the most successful approaches used to convince you to buy products?

Advertising Techniques

Everybody Uses It

Everyone is drinking Gulp, the new cola.

The Numbers Game

Four out of five people drink Gulp.

Famous People

The world's greatest athletes always drink Gulp.

Exaggeration

Gulp tastes the best.

Promises

Drink new Gulp, and you will feel energized!

Implication

If you serve Gulp at your next party, you will be a big hit!

Activities

Use the techniques listed above for the following activities.

- Using magazines and newspapers, find examples of each technique. Share your findings with the class.
- View a few different types of television shows. Record what is advertised and the advertising technique that is used.
- Listen to three different types of radio programs. Record what is being advertised and the technique that is used.
- Compare the types of advertisements and the advertising approaches that were used on television or the radio and in newspapers or magazines. Is there any one technique that is used most? Least? Share this information with the class.

50

Sell It Like It Is! *(cont.)*

If an inventor came to you for advertising assistance with his/her new invention, how would you promote the new product?

Below is a list of familiar inventions. Choose one item. Collect newspaper and magazine advertisements about the item.

Next, choose two different techniques of advertising. (See page 50 for techniques.) Design and write two different advertisements about the product you chose. In your ad, include information about how this product changes people's lives.

Invention List

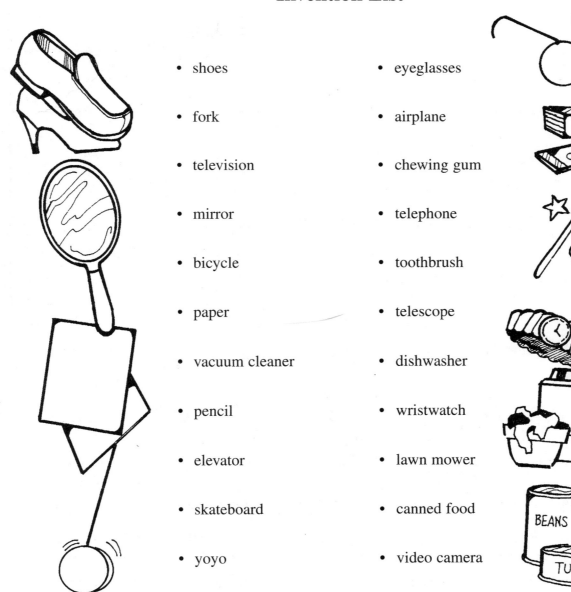

* shoes

* fork

* television

* mirror

* bicycle

* paper

* vacuum cleaner

* pencil

* elevator

* skateboard

* yoyo

* eyeglasses

* airplane

* chewing gum

* telephone

* toothbrush

* telescope

* dishwasher

* wristwatch

* lawn mower

* canned food

* video camera

When Did That Happen?

Below you will find the names and dates of several important inventions in history. Cut out the boxes and glue them to a time line that displays the information chronologically in an easy-to-understand fashion.

1920s television	1826 photography
1952–1955 polio vaccine	1849 safety pin
1983 compact disc	1902 air conditioning
3000 B.C. wheel	1940s tape recorder
1846 sewing machine	1876 telephone
1608 telescope	1804 steam locomotive
1903 airplane	1100s magnetic compass
1893 zipper	1,750,000 B.C. flint tools
1920s frozen foods	1793 cotton gin
1945 atomic bomb	1890s motion picture
100 B.C. paper	1867 dynamite

Challenge: Add the names and dates of other important inventions to your time line.

Time Line Math

Use your time line or the information provided on page 52 to answer the following math problems.

1. How many years after the invention of the telephone was the atomic bomb invented?

   _____

2 What was invented first: paper, the wheel, or flint tools?

   _____

3. How many years ago was the steam locomotive invented?

   _____

4. Add the numbers of the years the airplane, the cotton gin, and the safety pin were invented.

   _____

5. How many years after paper was the sewing machine invented?

   _____

6. The telescope was invented in 1608. Use the digits, 1, 6, 0, and 8 to arrive at the number 40. You may add, subtract, multiply, or divide the numbers.

   _____

7. The compact disc was invented in 1983. Use the digits, 1, 9, 8, and 3 to arrive at the number 24. You may add, subtract, multiply, or divide the numbers.

   _____

8. The zipper was invented in 1893. How many decades ago was that? How many years are left over?

   _____

9. Frozen foods were invented in the 1920s. How much would four frozen dinners cost, if each one was $2.50?

   _____

10. Television was also invented in the 1920s. If your favorite show comes on at 8:30 PM, and it is 11:00 AM now, how many hours do you have to wait for your show?

   _____

If My Calculator Could Talk!

Imagine life without a little invention known as the calculator! We all know how handy calculators are to add, subtract, multiply, and divide numbers; but did you know they can also "talk"?

Read the story below. Each time you come to a math problem, enter it in your calculator. Then turn your calculator upside down and read the word. Write the word in the blank. When you are done, try to invent your own calculator story.

_____, I'm your calculator. I want to tell you about the
140 ÷ 10

funniest thing I ever did _____. I hope I can tell it without
500 -165

starting to _____.
370,000 + 9,919

MR

Once, _____ , _____ , and _____ were using me to
118 + 99   15436 ÷ 2   (9 X 33) + 40

_____ if they had enough money to go to the _____.
67 x 5   .2 ÷ 10

_____was eating an _____ and he dropped the
7518 + 200   2979 ÷ 3

–

_____ all over the floor. Just then a _____ flew over
386,725 ÷ 5   (150 X 2) + 38

and was about to sting _____ on the _____. Her cat,
(50 X 4) + 17   237 + 400

_____ , came running down the _____and started to
35,563 + 2,175   15428 ÷ 2

+

_____ the _____ . But then _____ saw the
378408 + 401   1,690 ÷ 5   40, 000 – 2262

_____ _____ on the floor. She spit out the _____
1,000 – 7   15469 x 5   169 x 2

and ate the _____ instead.
7734.5 x 10

=

_____ that was funny!
9 x 501

54

Who's Responsible for This?

Find out about some important inventors by solving the problems below.

Each number in the sentences stands for a different letter. Use the key to help you. In each word, there are some math problems to solve in order to find the correct number.

1. Thomas $\underset{22}{E}\ \underset{23}{D}\ \underset{3\times6}{I}\ \underset{8}{S}\ \underset{12}{O}\ \underset{13}{n}$ invented the motion-picture camera and projector.

2. Orville and Wilbur $\underset{4}{W}\ \underset{9}{R}\ \underset{18}{I}\ \underset{5\times4}{G}\ \underset{19}{H}\ \underset{21\div3}{T}$ made the first successful airplane flight.

3. In 1960, Theodore H. $\underset{2\times7}{M}\ \underset{13\times2}{A}\ \underset{18}{I}\ \underset{14}{M}\ \underset{26}{A}\ \underset{13}{N}$ demonstrated the first laser.

4. In the mid 1400's, Johannes $\underset{20}{G}\ \underset{48\div8}{U}\ \underset{7}{T}\ \underset{22}{E}\ \underset{13}{N}\ \underset{25}{B}\ \underset{30-8}{U}\ \underset{9}{R}\ \underset{20}{G}$ invented printing as we know it today.

5. George $\underset{32\div8}{W}\ \underset{26}{A}\ \underset{8}{S}\ \underset{19}{H}\ \underset{40-22}{I}\ \underset{13}{N}\ \underset{20}{G}\ \underset{7}{T}\ \underset{12}{O}\ \underset{13}{N}\ \ \underset{8\times3}{C}\ \underset{26}{A}\ \underset{9}{R}\ \underset{5}{V}\ \underset{22}{E}\ \underset{15-6}{R}$

   developed hundreds of useful products from peanuts.

6. In 1926, Robert $\underset{20}{G}\ \underset{3\times4}{O}\ \underset{23}{D}\ \underset{23}{D}\ \underset{13+13}{A}\ \underset{9}{R}\ \underset{23}{D}$, who is considered the father of modern

   rocketry, launched the first liquid-fueled rocket.

7. The piano was invented in Italy in 1709 by Bartolommeo

   $\underset{6\times4}{\rule{1.5em}{0.4pt}}\ \underset{9}{\rule{1.5em}{0.4pt}}\ \underset{18}{\rule{1.5em}{0.4pt}}\ \underset{8}{\rule{1.5em}{0.4pt}}\ \underset{14\div2}{\rule{1.5em}{0.4pt}}\ \underset{12}{\rule{1.5em}{0.4pt}}\ \underset{3\times7}{\rule{1.5em}{0.4pt}}\ \underset{12}{\rule{1.5em}{0.4pt}}\ \underset{9}{\rule{1.5em}{0.4pt}}\ \underset{30-12}{\rule{1.5em}{0.4pt}}$.

8. The saxophone was patented by Adolphe $\underset{4\times2}{S}\ \underset{13+13}{A}\ \underset{3}{X}$ in 1846.

9. Edward $\underset{17}{J}\ \underset{11+11}{E}\ \underset{13}{N}\ \underset{8+5}{N}\ \underset{22}{E}\ \underset{3\times3}{R}$ discovered the smallpox vaccine.

10. Samuel $\underset{7\times2}{M}\ \underset{12}{O}\ \underset{9}{R}\ \underset{20-12}{S}\ \underset{22}{E}$ invented the telegraph.

Key

A= 26			T= 7
B= 25	H= 19	N= 13	U= 6
C= 24	I= 18	0= 12	V= 5
D=23	J= 17	P= 11	W=4
E= 22	K= 16	Q= 10	X= 3
F= 21	L= 15	R= 9	Y= 2
G=20	M=14	S= 8	Z= 1

Extension: Find out more about these inventors.

Circuit Folder Game

Benjamin Franklin was one of the first persons to experiment with electricity. He is famous for his 1752 kite-flying experiments in which he proved that lightning was electricity. Franklin's invention of the lightning rod saved many structures from damage and demonstrated how electricity flows through a good conductor. A conductor is a material that allows electrons to move easily through it. Most metals are good conductors of electricity.

Students can make a circuit board game by using the same idea that Ben Franklin had in mind when he invented the lightning rod.

For each circuit folder game you will need the following materials:

one 10" x 12" (25 cm x 30 cm) sheet of aluminum foil; one 9" x 12" (23 cm x 30 cm) file folder (no pockets); masking tape; hole punch; scissors; 3" x 5" (8 cm x 13 cm) sticky note paper; markers; one "D" battery; one flashlight bulb and porcelain socket (available at a hardware store); screwdriver; three 6" (15 cm) lengths of insulated copper bell wire

Directions

1. Assemble the bulb, battery, and wire portion of the circuit folder game using the diagram below.

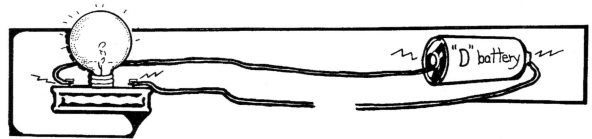

2. Cut the aluminum foil into five 2" x 12" (5 cm x 30 cm) strips. Fold up each strip lengthwise into thirds.

3. Face the file folder horizontally in front of you. Starting 2" (5 cm) from the top of the folder and about 1" in from the fold, punch a set of five holes in a column down the folder, spacing them about 2" (5 cm) apart. (You can keep the folder closed and punch through the top and bottom. Then use masking tape to cover the holes on the back of the folder.)

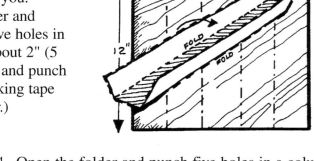

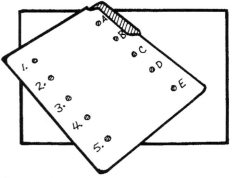

4. Open the folder and punch five holes in a column along the right side of the front cover 1" (2.54 cm) in from the edge and 2" apart, as you did on the left side. The two sets of holes should look the same on both sides of the folder cover.

5. Number the holes on the left from 1 to 5. Letter the holes on the right from A to E.

Circuit Folder Game *(cont.)*

Directions *(cont.)*

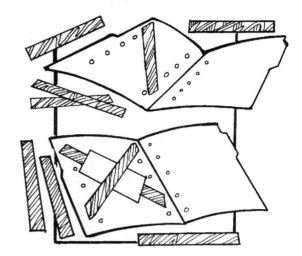

6. Open the folder. Place a folded strip of aluminum foil on the inside front cover over one of the holes in the left column and one of the holes in the right column. Tape it down. Cut off the excess foil.

7. Put another foil strip across a hole in each column. Before taping it down, put a sticky note over the first piece of foil so that no part of one foil strip comes in contact with another. (This provides insulation for the foil strip so that when you use your circuit folder you will be sure to complete an electrical circuit and light the bulb correctly.)

8. Continue adding the remaining foil strips as in steps 6 and 7. On the back of the folder draw a diagram that shows how you connected the foil strips from the left column to the right column. Use this as an answer key for a matching game.

9. Close the folder. Have each student invent a matching game in which items from the left column match their foil-strip connections in the right column. Write the match-up information on small pieces of sticky note paper and place them in the correct columns.

10. Ask students to exchange their folders and attempt to correctly match up the information from each column. When a student thinks he/she has a match, he or she places the bare wire ends over the holes. If the wires are placed on the foil inside the correct holes, the electric circuit will be completed and the bulb will light up.

Extension Ideas

• Students can change the game as many times as they like by replacing the match-up information on the sticky notes with new information. (Be sure that students use their answer keys to match the correct holes each time.)

• Circuit folder games can be used to study new information, make up riddles, solve math problems, etc.

• Make several folder games (or have students prepare additional ones) and place them at a center for students to use.

• Add more holes in each column of the folder so that students can match more items.

Tuned In

When Thomas Edison invented the phonograph in the late 1800s, he had no idea of the far-reaching effect of his invention. Audio technology has come a long way since the days of the phonograph.

Radio was first invented at about the same time as the phonograph, but was not perfected until the 1920s.

The radio became so popular that by the 1930s and 1940s people not only listened to it, but actually watched it in their minds. This was known as the "golden age of radio." News, music, adventure stories, comedies and variety shows, mysteries, and detective dramas could be heard on the radio.

Soon toy companies were making crystal radios. These only received a few stations and used a crystal radio antenna to pick up a signal from a transmitting station. You can build a simple crystal radio using the following materials and directions. (To build your crystal radio, you will need to purchase a few electronic components at a store that carries radio parts.)

Building a Crystal Radio

Materials

- coarse sandpaper
- scissors
- wire stripper
- sharp pencil
- toilet paper tube

- 2 alligator clips
- a crystal earphone (with wire leads)
- germanium diode
- 35 feet (11 m) solid insulated wire (#22)
- rubber band

Directions

1. Cut and set aside two lengths of wire, each three feet (91 cm) long.
2. Use a scissor or pencil to punch three holes, one inch (2.54 cm) apart from each other, near one end of the tube. Number the holes 1, 2, and 3.
3. Use scissors or a wire stripper to strip one inch of insulation from the end of the 35' (11 m) length of wire. Put this end through hole 1.
4. Wind the rest of this length of wire around the tube so that the coil is one layer thick and packed tightly together. Punch a hole in the tube near the last turn of the wire, push the wire end into the tube, and bend it so that it does not come out of the tube.
5. Use sandpaper to rub off a strip of insulation along the length of the coiled wire.
6. Carefully strip the insulation from the wire leads of the earphone and put one of the wires into hole 1.
7. Strip both ends of a three-foot (1 m) length of wire. Push one end through hole 1. Twist together all three wire ends in hole 1.
8. Attach the diode by bending the wire ends and inserting one end in hole 2 and one end in hole 3. Put the other earphone wire end into hole 2 and twist it together with the diode wire end.

58

Tuned In *(cont.)*

Building a Crystal Radio (cont.)

9. Strip about five inches (13 cm) of wire from one end of the second three-foot length of wire. Push this end through hole 3 from the inside of the tube, stopping just short of the insulation. (The extra wire sticking out of the tube will serve as a tuning wire.)

10. Twist the diode wire on the inside, close to the insulation.

11. Attach alligator clips to the stripped, loose ends of the three-foot wires.

How To Use Your Crystal Radio

Your crystal radio will need to be connected to an antenna in order to tune in radio stations. Connect one of the alligator clips to a metal faucet, a copper water pipe, or other metal things around the home or school. Perhaps you have an old antenna that you could use. (You may need to attach both alligator clips to metal objects in order to receive a station.)

Now, put the earphone in your ear and listen for a hum. Move the tuning wire (the stripped end of wire from hole 3) across the bare strip of coiled wire on the tube until you hear a radio station. To secure the station, wrap a rubber band around the tube where the wire end contacted the station.

Helpful Hints

- Nighttime listening and tuning usually works best.

- Be sure that the wire connections inside the tube do not touch the other connections.

- Make adjustments in the placement of the tuning wire, antenna hook-up, connections, etc., to improve the conditions and increase the chances of receiving radio stations on your crystal radio.

- Remember, inventors are constantly altering their inventions to get the best possible results. Be patient!

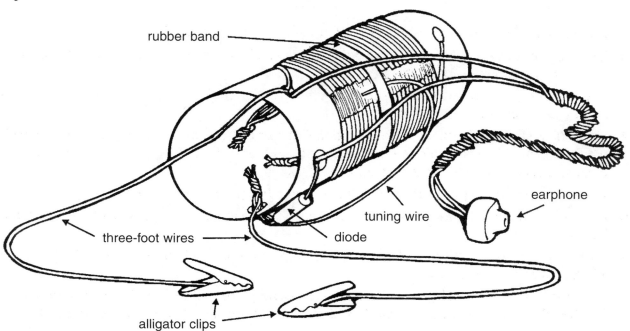

rubber band

three-foot wires

alligator clips

diode

tuning wire

earphone

Knot Then, Knot Now

The knot was invented thousands of years ago. Knots are used to join things together. They help us lift, pull, and support many things. Early man made traps and nets by knotting vines together. Primitive axes were constructed by tying a stone to a stick. Knots were believed to possess magical powers. In Rome, in the first century A.D., people believed injuries would heal faster if bandages were tied in a Hercules knot, now known as a reef knot. Knots were used to keep records in the culture of the Inca Indians of Peru.

Research to find out more about the history of the knot. Think about the following questions as you learn more about this simple but important invention:

- Why do you think the knot was invented?
- How has the knot improved life?
- In what other inventions does the knot play an important role?

Use a length of rope such as clothesline rope to make the knots below. In the last box, create your own knot, give it a name, and briefly describe how it might be used.

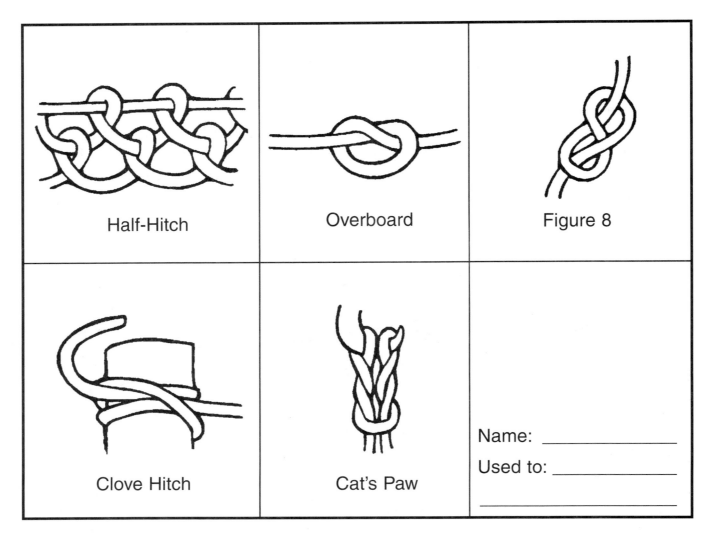

Half-Hitch	Overboard	Figure 8
Clove Hitch	Cat's Paw	Name: _____ Used to: _____ _____

Ask the Inventor

If you could interview an inventor from the past or present, who would you choose? The list of inventors below is only a small representation of the inventors who have made important contributions.

Choose an inventor from the list below (or select one of your own) and locate information that will help you complete the Inventor Research Sheet on page 62. Use the research information to write interview questions you might ask the inventor during an interview. Arrange an interview with a partner. Have your partner ask you the interview questions. Respond to them by using the information you learned through your research.

Inventor	*Invention*
Alexander Fleming	Penicillin
Wilhelm C. Roentgen	X-ray
Peter Hodgson	Silly Putty®
John Pemberton	Coca-Cola®
Spencer Silver	Post-it Notes®
Charles Goodyear	Vulcanization of Rubber
Vladimir Zworykin	Television
Howard Aiken	Computer
Leo Baekeland	Plastic
Robert Goddard	Rocket
Gordon Gould	Laser

Internet Extender

Museum of Ancient Inventions

http://www.smith.edu/hsc/museum/ancient_inventions/hsclist.htm

Activity Summary: View pictures of reconstructions made by college students of ancient inventions such as the catapult, ship shaker, and compass. Click on the picture to read more information about the invention. Click on Begin the Tour at the bottom of the page to see enlargements of all the pictures and full explanations. Have the students create their own reconstruction of an invention.

Inventor Research Sheet

Inventor's Name _____

Date of Birth/Death _____

Describe the inventor's early life. _____

_____

_____

_____

Describe the inventor's education and career. _____

_____

_____

_____

What was the inventor's most important contribution? _____

_____

_____

_____

Explain what the inventor's most famous invention does._____

_____

_____

_____

_____

_____

Be a Sport

What are some of your favorite sports? Behind every sport is a person or persons who created the game. Basketball was invented by a teacher, James Naismith, in 1891. The head of his school's Physical Education Department asked him to invent a game that could be played inside because the winters were too cold to participate in outdoor activities. He used a soccer ball and two goals made from peach baskets, which were attached to the balcony in the gym.

The invention of baseball is not as easy to trace. Most people believe the game was invented by Abner Doubleday in 1839 in Cooperstown, NY; however, historians believe it developed from a game called Rounders which was played in England as early as the 1600s.

Here's your chance to invent a new sport or a variation on an old one. You may decide what equipment to use for your game. The equipment listed below may give you some ideas. After you have invented your game, share it with your class and try it out. Write up the rules to the game in a class book. Be sure to include in the rules such information as how many players and teams can play, the equipment necessary, specific directions about how the game is played, and how the winner is determined.

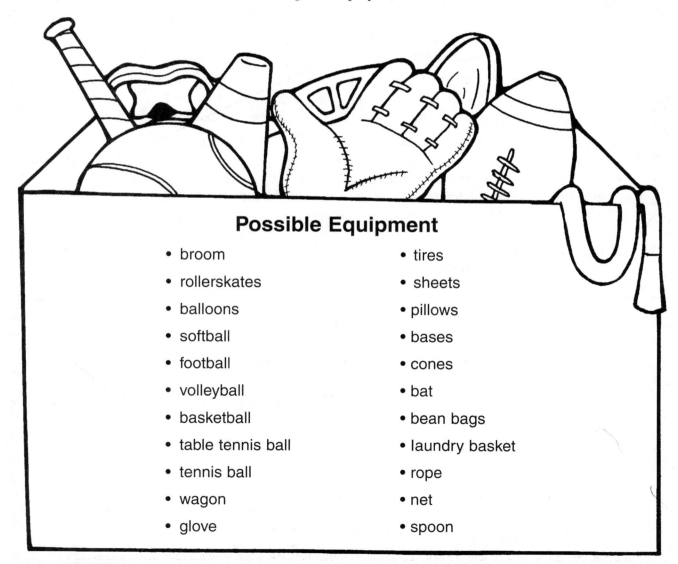

Possible Equipment

- broom
- rollerskates
- balloons
- softball
- football
- volleyball
- basketball
- table tennis ball
- tennis ball
- wagon
- glove

- tires
- sheets
- pillows
- bases
- cones
- bat
- bean bags
- laundry basket
- rope
- net
- spoon

A Frozen Delight

Many inventions come about as a result of finding solutions to big and little problems. After lots of experimentation with ingredients and techniques, Christian K. Nelson came up with a wonderful frozen delight called the Eskimo Pie®.

Here is a chance to invent a frozen delight of your own. Work with a partner to prepare the basic ice cream recipe below. Then, add some tasty ingredients to it. You could change the flavor as well. Be sure to use only healthy, safe food ingredients. When you are done, enjoy your tasty new invention!

Materials: one 3-pound (1.35 kg) coffee can lid; one 1 pound (.45 kg) coffee can and lid; water; crushed ice; rock salt; wire whisk; masking tape

Ingredients: one cup (240 mL) whipping cream; one cup (240 mL) milk; ½ cup (120 mL) sugar; ½ teaspoon (2.5 mL) vanilla, or your own choice of flavoring

Directions

1. Mix the ice cream ingredients in the one pound (.45 kg) coffee can. Securely tape the lid on the one pound coffee can.

2. Put a thin layer of crushed ice on the bottom of the three pound (1.35 kg) coffee can and sprinkle rock salt over the ice.

3. Place the one pound can inside the three pound can. Pack layers of ice and rock salt around the smaller can until the larger can is full. Put the lid on the larger can and seal it with tape.

4. Find a space on the floor where you and your partner can sit five feet (about 2 meters) apart. Choose an area that can be easily cleaned in case of leakage. Roll the coffee can back and forth for 15 minutes. Check to see if the ice cream has formed by taking the one pound can out and shaking it. If there is no sloshing, the ice cream is done. Add the ingredients (fruit chunks, nuts, etc.) you have chosen for your frozen delight. Spoon the ice cream into cups and enjoy it.

In the box below, illustrate the ingredients you added to the basic ice cream recipe. Write a brief explanation of how your invention turned out.

Ingredients

It's Instrumental

A successful inventor looks at an object and sees that it can have more than one function. Several glasses filled with different levels of water can serve as a musical scale for playing a favorite song.

Create a new instrument using materials commonly found around the home or at school. Decide how you will assemble them to make an instrument that will produce a sound. Draw your design in the box below. Label the parts of the instrument. At the bottom of the page, write a brief explanation of how to play your instrument.

Share your instrument invention with the class. Or, combine several instrument inventions to form your own band!

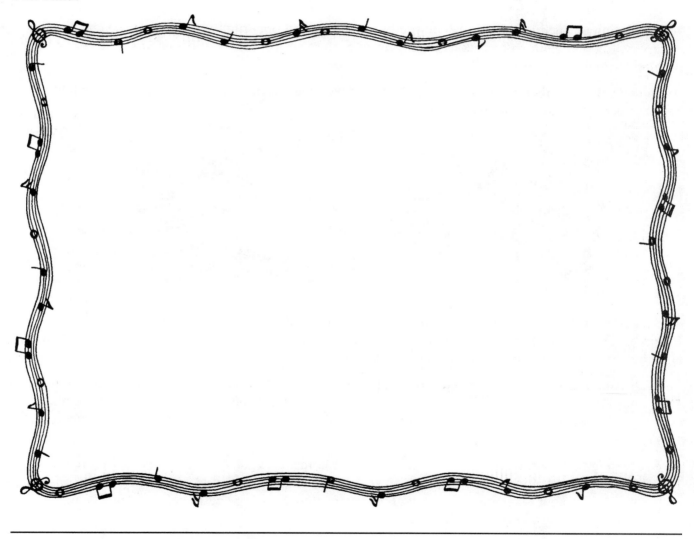

_____

_____

_____

_____

The Invention Connection

Introduction

The following pages are designed to help students experience firsthand the processes involved in the creation of a new invention, from the brainstorming of a new idea, through the design and completion of a model, and into the patent and marketing phases.

Students will be asked to invent a new product or improve on an existing idea. Have students use pages 68–78 as a resource and guide as they develop their inventions.

Preparation

The Invention Connection should be viewed by students as an opportunity to use their imagination and creativity. Encourage them to seek assistance from each other as they work cooperatively to solve the problems which may arise.

As students develop their ideas, remember that the invention experience is more important than the performance of the invention itself.

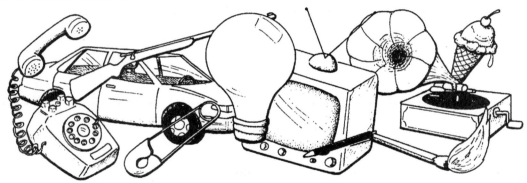

The suggestions below will help you prepare the students and the classroom environment for The Invention Connection. Since students will plan, prepare, and display their inventions, set aside times and physical space in which to work on the activities.

- Distribute pages 68–78 to each student. Have students cut out the cover (page 68). Make a folder out of a piece of construction paper or use a file folder. Glue the cover to the front of the folder. Attach the remaining pages inside. Students should complete the pages as they develop their inventions.

- Creating the inventions can be done at school, at home, or a combination of both. Before you introduce the students to the actual process involved in inventing, it is advisable to share information about inventions in general. Use the activity on page 67 to help students begin thinking like an inventor.

- Invite other classes, parents, and perhaps other members of the community to view the inventions on a specific day. Directions for a pop-up invitation are provided on page 78. Students should be encouraged to share their inventions with guests.

- Where possible, provide resources that students may require.

- When completed, the folders can be displayed along with the inventions. Students can also refer to the information they have collected as they share their inventions with others.

The Invention Connection *(cont.)*

Invention "Warm Up"

An invention is something that happens as a result of someone trying to solve a problem or situation with which he or she is not content. Inventions are made by people and help make life a little easier and/or quicker.

Have students brainstorm a list of things that are common in a house or at school. Ask if these things were made by people or by nature. Discuss how the items they listed served to make their lives or jobs easier.

Sometimes inventions are used in more ways than originally intended. Have students brainstorm the uses of a pencil. Discuss the suggestions.

Inventions affect history. Ask students if they could ever imagine what it would be like to have no television set in the home. Discuss how inventions change our lives. As an extension, ask students to interview an older person and find out about an invention that changed the older person's life. Ask the students to draw a "before" and "after" picture of the person and the invention and what the change looked like. Bring the pictures back the next day for discussion and feedback.

Internet Extender

Toys Were Us

http://www.discovery.com/stories/history/toys/toys.html

Activity Summary: This is a fun Web site which describes how such toys as the Barbie, Frisbee, Silly Putty, and Hula Hoop were invented. Assign students in groups to check out a different toy and then report back to the class about how it was created. Follow this by having them invent their own new toy, including giving it a name.

Invention Store

http://www.inventing.com/

Activity Summary: This Web site lists many inventions which have been picked up by manufacturers, as well as those still waiting for investors. After visiting this Web site and investigating several of the inventions, have the students create their own invention.

Young Inventors Program and Fair

http://www.ecsu.k12.mn.us/yif/index.html

Activity Summary: This Web site describes a Young Inventors Fair conducted through the Science Museum of Minnesota. Detailed information about this program can serve as a model to set up a similar fair at other schools. People involved in this program can be contacted online.

My Invention Book

by _____

I, _____,

intend to invent

_____
(Idea or Title)

because _____

How it will work: _____

_____

_____

_____

The supplies I will need: _____

_____

_____

_____

Teacher Approval: _____

Signed: _____ Date: _____

Steps to Inventing

1. Brainstorm ideas for it.

2. Plan and design it.

    Breadboard

    Model

    Prototype

3. Name it.

4. Patent it.

5. Give it a trademark.

6. Market it.

The Breadboard

An important step in planning how you will develop your invention and what it will look like is to create a breadboard. As an inventor, you will need to show that your invention can work.

In order to do this, you must present a rough, first construction of the invention. This is called a breadboard. Since it is still "in the rough," the materials and appearance do not have to resemble the finished, working model. You simply have to show that the idea of the invention works.

Gather materials for your invention. Assemble them to show the function of your invention. Do not be concerned if the parts don't work yet.

In the box below, draw a picture of your breadboard. Label the important parts.

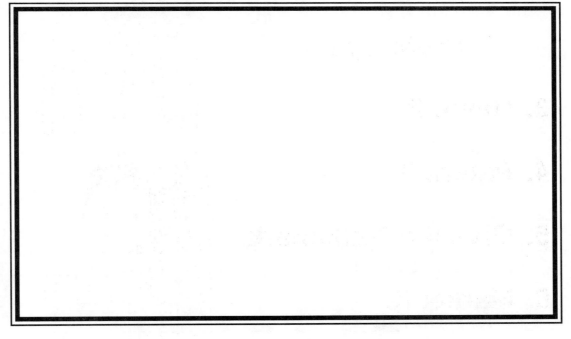

On the back of this page, write about how your idea (invention) will work.

The Model

Once you have made the breadboard, you are ready for the next step—the model. While planning the model, you need to think about more than the invention itself. An inventor considers the questions below as he or she starts a model. Try to answer each of them as an inventor might, keeping in mind the consumer who will buy your invention.

1. To what type of consumer will your invention appeal? _____
   _____

2. What special features will your invention have to attract consumers? _____
   _____

3. What do you think it will cost to produce your invention? _____
   _____

4. How much do you think you should sell your invention for? _____
   _____

5. Where will you sell your invention—in a catalog, at retail stores, etc.? _____
   _____

6. How will you package your invention? _____
   _____

7. If your invention is an improvement on a previous one, in what way is it better?
   If your invention is a brand new product, in what way is it unique?_____
   _____
   _____

72

The Prototype

The prototype is the next step in the development of your invention. It is usually a handmade sample that looks and performs exactly like the finished product. Inventors who want to produce and sell the invention themselves often choose to make a prototype to present to those who may be interested in buying the product.

Make a prototype of your invention. Then, take a photograph of it and glue or tape it in the box below. Fill in the blank at the bottom of the page.

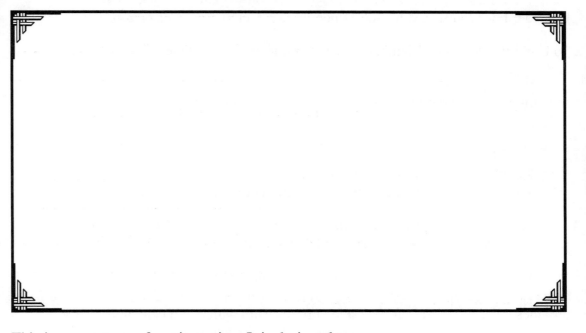

This is a prototype of my invention. It is designed to _____

_____

_____

_____

What's in a Name?

Now that you have planned and designed your invention, it is time to choose a name for your invention. Don't underestimate the importance of a product's name. Think about the advertisements and commercials you have seen. Which ones impress you the most? A product name will probably get your attention if it is catchy, easy to remember, funny, unusual, or clever. The name of an invention can help the inventor or manufacturer sell it!

Keep these ideas in mind as you brainstorm possible names for your invention. Consider how you would like other people to remember your invention.

To begin the process of naming your invention, think about the following questions and suggestions.

In naming your invention, do you want people to "connect" your invention to:

- your name?
- some part(s) of your invention?
- a unique feature of the invention?
- an acronym (where each letter in the product name stands for a word)?

Think of a brief descriptive phrase that explains what your invention is designed to do. Using your description, brainstorm a one, two, or three word title for your invention.

You may want to create a catchy name by adding a common prefix or suffix to the name of your invention, such as "Vivi-Tek Binoculars." *Steven Caney's Invention Book* provides a list of several prefixes and suffixes from which you can choose an invention name. Here are some common prefixes and suffixes:

Prefixes		**Suffixes**	
hydro-	uni-	-tric	-onic
hermo-	dyna-	-matic	-tron
tele-	bi-	-flex	-izer
multi-	auto-	-trac	-pedic
insti-	infra-	-etic	-ical
poly-	trans-	-atric	-tech
vege-	hyper-	-tek	-atric
centi-	super-	-tion	

Write the name of your invention here: _____

The Patent

A patent is a kind of trade agreement between the United States Government and the inventor. With this agreement, the inventor must publicize his/her invention, allowing other inventors to learn from the new invention and/or improve upon their own inventions. The government then protects the inventor by giving him or her "exclusive" permission to manufacture and sell the invention.

If an inventor decides to patent an invention, he or she then applies for the patent. Fill out the patent application below. Ask two witnesses to sign it.

Patent Application

Name of Invention: _____

Description of Invention: _____

Attach a sketch of your invention:

I, _____, affirm that I am the original and first

inventor of the _____.

Signed: _____

Witness:_____

Witness:_____

Office of Patents and Trademarks

Whereas, there has been presented to the Office of Patents and Trademarks on

this _____ day of _____ in the year
       (date)   (month)

_____, petition for a new invention titled

_____,

the said inventor, _____,

is granted this patent under the law.

This Letter Patent hereby grants to the inventor, _____,

the right to exclude all other persons from using, selling, or

making the aforementioned invention.

Signature _____

Office of Patents and Trademarks

The Trademark

Many companies distinguish their products from those of another company by using trademarks, also called brand names. The trademark can be a symbol, a name, a word or group of words, a picture, a design, or even a sound. Trademarks usually appear in advertisements and/or on the product itself. A trademark makes it easy to identify a product; and if a consumer is pleased with the product, he or she is likely to purchase another with the same brand name in the future.

In the box below, design a trademark that you would like to have represent your invention.

Pop-Up Invitation

Materials: 9" x 12" (23 cm x 30 cm) white construction paper (two pieces per student); glue; crayons; colored pencils or markers; scissors; rulers; paper for making a pop-up pattern

Directions

1. Have students fold a piece of paper in half and cut a slit on the fold 3" (8 cm) in from each edge. Make slits about 2" (5 cm) long.

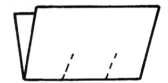

2. Open the fold, push it through, and crease it to form a pop-up section.

3. Fold the second piece of construction paper in half and glue it to the first as shown. This becomes the front and back of the invitation. Have students decorate the invitation cover.

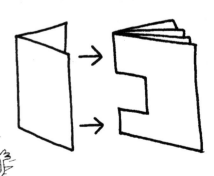

4. Reproduce the pattern on page 80. Have students color the pattern and glue it to the pop-up section as shown.

Note: Work with students on the details to be included on the inside (bottom section) of the invitation.

78

Bibliography

Aaseng, Nathan. *The Inventors.* Lerner Publications, 1988.

——*Twentieth Century Inventors.* Facts on File, 1991.

Bendick, Jeanne. *Eureka! It's an Airplane!* Millbrook, 1992.

Boesen, Victor. *William P. Lear.* Hawthorne Books, Inc., 1974.

Caney, Steven. *Steven Caney's Invention Book.* Workman Publishing, 1985.

Cousins, Margaret. *Thomas Alva Edison.* Random House, 1965.

Crump, Donald J. *Small Inventions that Make a Big Difference.* National Geographic, 1984.

D'Aulaire. *Benjamin Franklin.* Doubleday & Company, 1965.

Davidson, Margaret. *Louis Braille.* Hastings House, 1971.

Dempsey, Michael. *Growing up with Science: The Illustrated Encyclopedia of Invention.* Stuttman, 1987.

Eichner, James. *Thomas Jefferson.* Franklin Watts, Inc., 1966.

——*Those Inventive Americans.* National Geographic, 1971.

Getz, David. *Almost Famous.* Holt, 1992.

Graham, Ian. *Inventions.* Bookwright Press, 1987.

Groves, Seli and Dian Buchman. *What If? Fifty Discoveries That Changed the World.* Scholastic, 1988.

Gunston, Bill. *Coal.* Franklin Watts, 1981.

Hayden, Robert. *Eight Black American Inventors.* Addison-Wesley, 1972.

Jeffries, Michael and Gary A. Lewis. *Inventors and Inventions.* Smithmark, 1992.

Jeunesse, Gallimard. *Airplanes and Flying Machines.* Cartwheel, 1992.

Lawson, Robert. *Ben and Me.* Little, Brown and Company, 1988.

Manchester, Harland. *New Trail Blazers of Technology.* Charles Scribner's Sons, 1976.

Murphy, Jim. *Weird & Wacky Inventions.* Crown Publishers, 1978.

O'Sullivan, Tom. *The World's Greatest Inventors.* Platt and Munk, 1976.

Pape, Donna Lugg. *Foolish Machinery.* Scholastic Inc., 1988.

Pratt, Fletcher. *All About Famous Inventors and Their Inventions.* Random House, 1955.

Richards, Norman. *Dreamers & Doers: Inventors Who Changed the World.* Macmillan, 1984.

Robbin, Irving. *Basic Inventions.* Charles E. Merrill Books, Inc., 1965.

Russell, Solveig. *Everyday Wonders.* Parents Magazine Press, 1973.

Smith, David and Sue Cassin. *The Amazing Book of Firsts—Great Ideas.* Mallard Press, 1990.

Spier, Peter. *Bored—Nothing to Do!* Doubleday, 1978.

Sullivan, George. *More How Do They Make.* Westminster Press, 1969.

Taylor, Barbara. *Be an Inventor.* Harcourt Brace Jovanovich, 1987.

Vare, Ethlie. *Mothers of Invention.* William Morrow and Company, 1988.

Weiss, Harvey. *How to Be an Inventor.* Crowell, 1980.

Wulffson, Don. *Invention of Ordinary Things.* Avon Books, 1981.

Answer Key

Page 15
1. answer given ($2.00)
2. $.40
3. answer given ($1.00)
4. $.25
5. $.50
6. $2.50

Page 25
1. 2 adults, 16 children; 1 adult, 18 children; 0 adults, 20 children
2. 100 pieces
3. $52.50
4. yes. $2.75 leftover
5. yes

Pages 27 and 28
1. behind
2. healthy, wealthy, & wise
3. a penny earned
4. live to eat
5. dead
6. two tomorrows
7. doers
8. no mice
9. well said
10. with tongue

Page 30
One way is to "charge" the comb and pass it over the salt and pepper mixture. The pepper will cling to the comb. Accept any other appropriate responses.

Page 36
Braille letters should match these responses:
1. Levi Strauss
2. penicillin
3. Frisbee

Page 53
1. 69
2. Flint tools
3. Subtract 1804 from the current year.
4. 5,545
5. 1,946
6. [(6-1) + 0] x 8 = 40
7. [(1x9) x 8] ÷ 3 = 24
8. Subtract 1893 from current year and divide by 10.
9. $10.00
10. 9½ hours

Page 54
Hi, I'm your calculator. I want to tell about the funniest thing I ever did **see.** I hope I can tell it without starting to **giggle.**

Once, **Liz, Bill,** and **Lee** were using me to **see** if they had enough money to go the **zoo. Bill** was eating an **egg,** and he dropped the **shell** all over the floor. Just then a **bee** flew over and was about to sting **Liz** on the **leg.** Her cat, **Belle,** came running down the **hill** and started to **gobble** the **bee.** But then **Belle** saw the **egg shell** on the floor. She spit out the **bee** and ate the **shell** instead. **Gosh** that was funny!

Page 55
1. Edison
2. Wright
3. Maiman
4. Gutenberg
5. Washington Carver
6. Goddard
7. Cristofori
8. Sax
9. Jenner
10. Morse

Page 78
Cut out the pattern below and use it to make the Pop-Up Invitation on page 78.